"This book grabs the heart and grips the soul! Jan and Don teach us that we can take responsibility for our own lives and learn to live in intimate relationships with the people we love. This book will be a blessing to all who read it!"

— CYNTHIA SPELL HUMBERT, speaker, counselor, and author of *Deceived by Shame, Desired by God* (NavPress)

"Don and Jan have pulled from their own marriage endless examples of how we, with unclaimed baggage, can sort through our own histories. Eventually, you will be able to claim your baggage, sort out the clothing, and replace it in your closet in an orderly fashion. With God's help, we can claim our unclaimed baggage."

— EMILIE BARNES, author and speaker

UNCLAIMED BAGGAGE

Dealing with the Past on Your Way to a Stronger Marriage

DON AND JAN FRANK

BRINGING TRUTH TO LIFE
P.O. Box 35001, Colorado Springs, Colorado 80935

OUR GUARANTEE TO YOU

We believe so strongly in the message of our books that we are making this quality guarantee to you. If for any reason you are disappointed with the content of this book, return the title page to us with your name and address and we will refund to you the list price of the book. To help us serve you better, please briefly describe why you were disappointed. Mail your refund request to: NavPress, P.O. Box 35002, Colorado Springs, CO 80935.

The Navigators is an international Christian organization. Our mission is to reach, disciple, and equip people to know Christ and to make Him known through successive generations. We envision multitudes of diverse people in the United States and every other nation who have a passionate love for Christ, live a lifestyle of sharing Christ's love, and multiply spiritual laborers among those without Christ.

NavPress is the publishing ministry of The Navigators. NavPress publications help believers learn biblical truth and apply what they learn to their lives and ministries. Our mission is to stimulate spiritual formation among our readers.

ISBN 1-57683-358-5

Cover design by David Carlson
Cover illustration by Photonica / Ryo Konno
Creative Team: Nanci McAlister, Karen Lee-Thorp, Janel Breitenstein, Darla Hightower, Glynese Northam

Some of the anecdotal illustrations in this book are true to life and are included with the permission of the persons involved. All other illustrations are composites of real situations, and any resemblance to people living or dead is coincidental.

Unless otherwise identified, all Scripture quotations in this publication are taken from the HOLY BIBLE: NEW INTERNATIONAL VERSION® (NIV®). Copyright © 1973, 1978, 1984 by International Bible Society. Used by permission of Zondervan Publishing House. All rights reserved. Other versions used include: the *New American Standard Bible* (NASB), © The Lockman Foundation 1960, 1962, 1963, 1968, 1971, 1972, 1973, 1975, 1977; THE MESSAGE (MSG). Copyright © 1993, 1994, 1995, 1996, 2000, 2001, 2002. Used by permission of NavPress Publishing Group; and the *New King James Version* (NKJV). Copyright © 1982 by Thomas Nelson, Inc. Used by permission. All rights reserved.

Frank, Don.
  Unclaimed baggage : dealing with the past on your way to a stronger marriage / by Don and Jan Frank.
      p. cm.
Includes bibliographical references.
  ISBN 1-57683-358-5
  1. Marriage--Religious aspects--Christianity. I. Frank, Jan. II. Title.
  BV835 .F712 2003
  248.8'44--dc21
                                   2002151984

Printed in the United States of America

1 2 3 4 5 6 7 8 9 10 / 07 06 05 04 03

FOR A FREE CATALOG OF
NAVPRESS BOOKS & BIBLE STUDIES,
CALL 1-800-366-7788 (USA)
OR 1-416-499-4615 (CANADA)

To Jim and Pat Lancaster
whose love and marriage inspired me
at seventeen—and gave me hope.

And in loving memory of
Lillian M. Frank
1924-2001
whose love and laughter brought joy
to our hearts and home.
Tervetuloa kotiin
Näkemiin

TABLE OF CONTENTS

ACKNOWLEDGMENTS

DEEPEST GRATITUDE TO MY "FAST-TRACK" FRIENDS: Marian McFadden and Ginny Lukei. Let us continue to "run . . . the race marked out for us" together (Hebrews 12:1).

Heartfelt thanks to:

Our daughters: Kellie, who prays and helps from a servant's heart, and Heather, who has taught us about the depth of our Father's love.

My "spiritual moms," Pam Houston and Dotty Stephenson, whose intercession and e-mails lift my spirit and keep me focused.

My sweet friend Mae, who loves, prays, and encourages me with her laughter, amidst her own battle with cancer.

Praying friends: Daniel Fleeman, Dan and Dee Maltby, Steve and Marcia Penuel, Brian and Vicky Burgess, Don and Mary Pedrick, Jerry and Jenny Crossman, Kim Pennington, Teresa Coehlo, and many others who've prayed for this book to come to completion.

Patsy and Les Clairmont for their "desert nest"—a home away from home.

Special thanks to:

Heidi Matson, Jenni Key, and Paula Allaire for your editing skills and your insights. You helped me more than you know.

Judy Couchman and the Symposium women—thanks for cheering me on.

Nanci McAlister, acquisitions editor at NavPress, who believed in this book from the beginning. Thanks, Nanci, for not giving up!

Karen Lee-Thorp, whose editorial input challenged me and caused me to think beyond my limited scope. You are masterful in your craft!

Kim Curtis for her hard work on the illustration.

The NavPress family—thank you all for your unique gifts that contribute to producing material for the glory of God.

Many couples with whom we've shared—you have blessed our lives by sharing your journeys.

Our gracious God and faithful Father, whose mercies "are new every morning" (Lamentations 3:23).

CHAPTER I

THE IMPORTANCE
OF YOUR HISTORY

A MONTH AND A HALF AFTER WE MOVED INTO OUR DREAM home, Don woke in the middle of the night to some strange noises. He got out of bed to investigate. From the upstairs bathroom he yelled, "We have a flood!" The toilet was shooting a stream of water over the bathroom. Even after he turned off the water supply line, everything was soaked. His feet sank into the carpet with a sloshing sound.

When I met him on the stairway, he wailed, "Everything is ruined — our house, our new house!" We embraced and prayed. "Lord," I said, "I *know* You gave us this house, and even though we don't understand, we're going to trust You. I know this is no accident. You knew it would happen because You're sovereign and You're in control. Please help us in this situation and in some way redeem this."

Within minutes of our call, the fire department was at our door. They vacuumed up forty-five gallons of water from our downstairs family room, hallway, bath, and den. It made no difference because water still poured through a light fixture in our downstairs bathroom. The ceiling in our den, directly below the upstairs bathroom, threatened to give way. We guessed that earlier in the week, the plumber had hooked up the water supply line improperly. The line had blown off, causing hundreds of gallons of water to seep through the walls, floor, and ceiling for four hours and damaging almost the whole house. We had suffered significant losses that required extensive repair.

A friend told me about a man in our church named Brad who was in the "restoration business." I didn't know such companies existed. I called Brad and, although he passed on the project, I learned what restoration companies do. They inspect a home that has suffered fire or flood and assess the damage, implement a plan of restoration, and at completion, return to the home-owner a home in better condition than the original.

The repairs on our house took the next six months. My life was consumed with contacting insurance companies, getting estimates, choosing new carpeting and wallpaper, coordinating schedules with workmen, and figuring out which repairs needed to be done first. It was a tedious process full of setbacks and unanticipated stress. We lived for six months on bare, cold concrete floors. When the carpet layers called to schedule installation, I realized we would be moving out of our house for the second time, only to move back in the same day. It was exhausting! It required so much mental energy that I couldn't even get excited about the "newness" that was enveloping us. I never would have chosen this.

But when it was finally over, I looked around at my new carpeting and wallpaper, newly painted rooms, and restored furniture in amazement. Out of this damaging interruption we had been given a fresh start. Our home was even better than when we purchased it, and the entire repair cost had been covered.

A FRESH START

Stunned, I saw that what we experienced in our home was analogous to what we had lived in our marriage. Don and I married unaware of our need for restoration. When we married over twenty-three years ago, we looked like the all-American couple. Both of us were committed Christians who loved each other and desired to establish our relationship on the principles outlined in God's Word. We wanted, as most couples do, a satisfying marriage, and we were dedicated to pursuing that goal. Neither of us had any idea that our backgrounds would play a significant role in shaping our marriage.

Both Don and I suffered some devastating losses in our lives before marriage. I was a sexual abuse victim. Don was an adult child of an alcoholic. We married with the knowledge of our backgrounds but were naïve about the effect they would have in the day-to-day working out of our marriage. We were unaware that our histories had anything to do with our present. We lived as though we had no histories, simply because we assumed that *our* history started when we got married.

We couldn't have been more wrong. We discovered through circumstances and strife that our histories were seeping into every room of our marriage "house." Our histories showed up in the kitchen each time we had a meal. They were in the bathroom when we got ready for work in the morning. And our histories flooded the bedroom, though we tried desperately to keep them from drowning our hopeful hearts.

DIVINE INTERRUPTIONS

At the time, these discoveries appeared to be damaging interruptions. In reality, God's loving grace was at work. Early in our marriage, He stepped in to change our direction. We would not have pursued that direction on our own, but now we're glad for it. God took us back to help us go forward.

Ours is a love story. God loved us enough to help us realize we could not go on in our relationship until we dealt honestly with our pasts. He loved us through the painful process of coming to grips with the losses, and He led us along the path of restoration. He provided abundant grace as we sought Him for healing and forgiveness. He patiently instructed us about how to build a strong foundation of love and faith. He took us back to our foundations, helping us do the necessary repair work and teaching us what it takes to maintain a healthy, satisfying marriage. We have a strong, loving marriage today. Although I (Jan) am telling most of the stories here in my voice, this book is very much our story. Don and I have walked this process together, and the insights we will share with you come out of our joint experience in our own marriage, in working with other couples in seminars and conferences, and in my private practice as a counselor.

God is in the restoration business! He gave us back something better than what we started with in the beginning.

I know many couples like us. You may be one of them. You may have married your mate unaware of how your history affects your relationship. You haven't assessed the damage, and you're living as if it had not happened. You may have thought, as we did, that your history began when you married. But this approach can be hazardous to the health of your marriage.

Imagine for a moment what would have happened after our flood if both Don and I regarded the damage in our home as insignificant. What if we had continued to walk around on the drenched carpeting and determined that all would work out in time if we did our best to go on? After a while, the weight of the saturated carpet upstairs might have caused the floor to cave in. Over time, the wood might have rotted. The mildew behind walls and under carpet might not have been visible, but the effect would have been inescapable. These conditions would have been harmful and potentially dangerous to all living in our home.

What if, instead of ignoring the damage, we had acknowledged it and had taken some initial steps of repair, but had found it required too much time and work? We might have removed the carpeting and fixed the water supply line but not bothered to repair the walls, floor, and furniture. We certainly could have adjusted to living on the cement slab, but I wonder what effect that would have had on our children or visitors? Because the repair had required more effort than we'd bargained for, would that have been reason enough to give up?

What if, instead of ignoring or giving up, we had denied that the flood had occurred at all? That would have been impossible — and dangerous.

How many couples do these very things! I know couples in all three categories! Some marry with histories of damage and try to live out their marriages without reckoning with what happened, not realizing the significance of their histories. Others take some initial steps of repair but become discouraged and abandon the continuous work toward restoration. They adjust to living in less than what God designed for marriage. Some refuse to believe that their histories affect their present and continue to live submerged by them.

WHAT ABOUT YOUR HISTORY?

Your history may not be full of devastation. It may not require rebuilding from the ground up. It may require only minor repairs, like replacing a water heater in your home. In such repairs, the time and effort required are minimal, but if you ignore them, life could be uncomfortable for years to come with cold showers and no running water!

All of us have histories that include both good and bad. Discomfort or disaster is inescapable if the history is left unheeded. If, however, that water heater or flood is attended to, lifelong distress or destruction can be averted. I'm so thankful that God exposed the overflow of our histories that had the potential to wash out our marriage.

UNCLAIMED BAGGAGE HISTORY

We all have both history and baggage. Our history is made up of the events and experiences that shape our lives. Our baggage is the emotional response to our history. Our emotional baggage may be claimed or unclaimed. What we claim is what we recognize as ours and deal with forthrightly. Unclaimed baggage is what we ignore, deny, or minimize.

If you've traveled through airports, you know that after deplaning, most travelers head for the baggage claim area to pick up their bags. You stand around a huge carousel, waiting for your bags to appear. Once you spot them, you pull them off and you're on your way.

Also in the baggage claim area are bags that are set aside because no one has claimed them. Every year the airlines accumulate hundreds of items that remain unclaimed. These are placed in a storage area and held for a prescribed time, waiting for their owners to claim them.

In counseling, I see many people who have areas in their lives where unclaimed baggage has been stored. They're often unaware that they carry a garment bag full of resentment over some unresolved hurt from a previous marriage. They may carry a duffle bag of depression over losing someone they loved, or an overnight case of doubt about God's love due to betrayals in their past. This unclaimed baggage history is like the faulty water heater or silent flood in the house. It has the potential to ruin a marriage if it is not claimed and dealt with.

Your history and the baggage you carry as a result are linked. When you marry, you come face-to-face with your partner's past as well as your own. Even though you cannot change your histories, with God's help you can learn to deal with the resulting baggage and build a stronger marriage. That is what this book is about. You will discover what makes up your history, the baggage that has resulted, what to do with it, how to distinguish whose baggage is whose, and how your history can actually enhance your relationship. You will find, as we did, that once you've claimed your baggage, you can unpack it, unload the burden of it from your marriage, and learn to travel lighter to the glory of God.

IS IT BIBLICAL TO LOOK BACK?

As a counselor, I have seen the impact of history played out over and over. Not just in the lives of individuals, but also in families. Certain patterns are transferred from one generation to the next. Who hasn't heard of families in which alcoholism or abuse runs rampant? What about adultery and greed? We learn about relationships within our families, and we pass on to our children what we learn if we don't give God access to change us.

Yet Christian premarital classes, books about marriage, and weekend marriage retreats often neglect to mention the role history plays in our marriages. Christians seem to resist looking into the past. It's almost as if we deny we have one. But Scripture admonishes us to "look to the rock from which you were hewn" (Isaiah 51:1, NASB), and provides countless examples of faith heroes whose past histories played significant roles in their present and future.

Consider the prophet Samuel. His mother dedicated him to the Lord's service, and when he was about three years old, she took him to Eli the priest. Eli raised Samuel and taught the boy the priestly duties.

Eli had two sons of his own, Hophni and Phineas, who were both priests. First Samuel 2:12 says, "Eli's sons were wicked men; they had no regard for the LORD." God spoke through Samuel as a young boy, and His message to Eli was, "For I [God] told him [Eli] that I would judge his family forever because of the sin he knew about; his sons made themselves contemptible, and he [Eli] failed to restrain them" (1 Samuel 3:13). Eli served the Lord faithfully as a priest and taught Samuel well in ways of the Lord, but fell down when it came to fathering his sons.

The Scripture goes on: "The LORD was with Samuel as he grew up, and he let none of his words fall to the ground. And all Israel from Dan to Beersheba recognized that Samuel was attested as a prophet of the LORD" (1 Samuel 3:19-20). Samuel was a great man of God as a prophet, intercessor, priest, and judge. All his prophecies came to pass: he interceded for Israel's great victory over the Philistines, he offered sacrifices to God for the people, and he provided judgment in both moral and spiritual matters all his life. However,

When Samuel grew old, he appointed his sons as judges of Israel. The name of his firstborn was Joel and the name of

his second was Abijah, and they served at Beersheba. But
his sons did not walk in his ways. They turned aside after
dishonest gain and accepted bribes and perverted justice.
(1 Samuel 8:1-3)

Sound familiar? Eli had taught Samuel in the ways of the Lord, but Samuel faltered, as did Eli, when it came to fatherhood.

"We cannot do what we have never seen done," write Drs. Henry Cloud and John Townsend in *How People Grow.* "We need models to show us how. . . . God designed humans with a need to see others first do what they need to learn, and then to internalize that modeling and be able to repeat it. The modeling we experience has a lasting effect upon us, for good or ill."[1]

Why did God include in His Word the tale of Samuel's failure as a father? Is this simply a recording of historical information, or is there something we can learn? What does the New Testament have to say regarding our history?

Think about the apostle Paul. He was a man with a history. How do we know about Paul's history? He wrote about it repeatedly. He recorded his history in 1 Corinthians 15:9; 2 Corinthians 11:24-33; Galatians 1:13-17; and Philippians 3:4-6. Luke wrote about Paul's history in Acts, reviewing his conversion and how Paul recounted his history before kings and crowds who opposed his message (Acts 22:3-11; 23:6; 24:10-21; 26:2-32).

You might be confused. Wasn't it Paul who wrote the verses that seem to indicate our past is gone and should be forgotten? What do we do with 2 Corinthians 5:17: "Therefore, if anyone is in Christ, he is a new creation; the old has gone, the new has come"? Or Philippians 3:13: "But one thing I do: Forgetting what is behind and straining toward what is ahead, I press on toward

the goal to win the prize for which God has called me heaven-
ward in Christ Jesus"?

What did Paul mean when he wrote these words?

- Did he mean you should wipe your history from your
  memory?
- Did he mean you should stay aware but push your his-
  tory down and not connect it to your present or future?
- Did he mean you should never talk about it?
- Did he mean it is no longer of any importance?[2]

I don't think he was saying any of the above. Instead, I think
Paul had a distinct understanding about his history and how God
wanted to use it.

Let's look in Philippians at what Paul said about his history:

> For it is we who are the circumcision, we who worship by
> the Spirit of God, who glory in Christ Jesus, and who put
> no confidence in the flesh—though I myself have reasons
> for such confidence. If anyone else thinks he has reasons to
> put confidence in the flesh, I have more: circumcised on the
> eighth day, of the people of Israel, of the tribe of Benjamin, a
> Hebrew of Hebrews; in regard to the law, a Pharisee; as for
> zeal, persecuting the church; as for legalistic righteousness,
> faultless. (Philippians 3:3-6, emphasis added)

Paul said we should not have *confidence* in our history—we
should not use it to claim a higher position. Today, having confidence in your history might mean saying that because your grandparents were the founding members of your church, your status in

the church should be higher than that of others. It might mean looking down on those who have a different ethnic heritage or social status. It might mean thinking you should have an advantage in society or the church because of your educational background. Paul would tell you not to regard your history in that way.

Is it possible that Paul meant *our histories are not to define us?*

Our histories should set us neither above nor below another. Our histories should not be the determining factor in who we are as believers — either by pride or by shame.

Paul focused on the pride side of this coin. I see the other side all too often: our histories become our shame. That's the opposite of what Paul was talking about, but it's no less defining.

Max Lucado contrasts these two robbers of our true identity in Christ:

> *Pride and shame. You'd never know they are sisters. They appear so different. Pride puffs out her chest. Shame hangs her head. Pride boasts. Shame hides. Pride seeks to be seen. Shame seeks to be avoided. But don't be fooled, the emotions have the same parentage. And the emotions have the same impact. They keep you from the Father. Pride says, "You're too good for Him." Shame says, "You're too bad for Him." Pride drives you away. Shame keeps you away. If pride is what goes before a fall, then shame is what keeps you from getting up after one.*[3]

We are not to live in pride or shame because of our histories. We are not to let our histories define us. We are to face our histories and then give them to God and let Him use them for His glory.

Paul told the Galatians that others were praising God because of his history. They knew that Paul, who had formerly persecuted the church, was "now preaching the faith he once tried to destroy" (Galatians 1:23). The contrast between his former life and his present one caused the church to offer praise to God. This is why our histories are important. They are the baseline from which change occurs. They are the basis of our testimony of God's grace at work in our lives.

I have known many Christians who have spent a lifetime ignoring, denying, or playing down their past. They've been misled to believe that somehow all of their histories were wiped out once they came to know Christ. Certainly our sins were blotted out when we trusted Christ as our personal Lord and Savior, and we stand justified before God on the basis of our faith in what Christ did for us on the cross. But our histories are not annihilated when we become believers.

Our histories are not an obstacle to God. In fact, I think He rather enjoys transforming them. He desires to "rebuild the ancient ruins and restore the places long devastated," bringing "beauty instead of ashes" to those who put their trust in Him. (Isaiah 61:4 ; 61:3). His plan of restoration does not mean we're supposed to forget the "ancient ruins" — annihilate them and never think about them again. Forgetting the past in that sense is no mark of spirituality. God neither ignores nor plays down our ruins.

If God doesn't ignore, deny, play down, or annihilate our histories, what does He do with them? He redeems them. He's the only One who can do that. This redemption means that He frees us from the consequences our histories invoke and uses our histories for His glory. No matter what they include, God is able to use them to bring us good and Him glory. But He does not do it in one fell swoop. He does it over time, just as He conforms us into

His image over time. It is not an immediate transformation but a process in which His Spirit is continually at work within us.

What is your part in the redemptive process as it relates to your history? It is threefold: recognition of your past, acceptance of His provision, and submission to His plan. Your part is voluntary. God usually will not muscle His way into areas in your life that you hold back from Him. He doesn't barge in where He is not wanted, but rather He stands at the door and knocks, waiting to be invited in. Maybe you have walled off your past, even for spiritual reasons. God will not pry you open. He gives you the choice. He may gently prod you by allowing you to experience consequences of your history, hoping that you will yield it to Him, but He will not force you to yield. You must do that on your own.

I like to think of it in terms of giving Him access. To give someone access to something means that we give him or her the permission or ability to enter or make use of whatever we are making accessible. We also give him the means by which access is obtained. It is a bit different than making something available. I may have a room available for rent in my home, but unless I give you the key, that availability is worthless.

The key to redeeming your history is in giving God access — fully and totally. By giving Him access, you give Him permission to enter it and make use of it as He desires. By denying Him access, you restrict the flow of His redemptive grace in your life. You can rightly give access only to something you own; therefore, you must claim your history before any restoration or redemption can occur.

Years after Paul's conversion he was still talking about his history. Why did he continue to mention it? He was free to do so and let God use his past to raise it to a realm of praise for the glory and honor of God.

BENEFITS OF HISTORY EXPLORATION

Still, you may be skeptical. You may be asking what possible benefit there is to looking back. Why spend time looking at something that cannot be changed? Isn't it a bit like "crying over spilt milk"?

It depends on how you look at "spilt milk." Some people look at spilt milk as an accident needing a quick remedy. They say, "Stop lamenting over the lost milk. Get a towel, clean it up, and pour yourself some more milk. Get on with your life." They think that it's a waste of time to wallow in something that can't be changed, and that with a little effort, life can and should go on unaffected by a single glass of "spilt milk."

But what if "spilt milk" is a daily occurrence? What if, for as long as you can remember, you have spilled your milk at mealtime? There are a couple of ways you might view this repetitive pattern: First, you might not be aware that this "pattern" exists because it has been with you for the last thirty-five years. Or, you might assume that spilling milk is normal because you have been doing it all your life, and in your family growing up, your father did the same thing. You might realize that a lot of milk has been spilled over the years, but you've seemed to manage just fine and you've learned always to keep an extra gallon of milk in the refrigerator.

Now let's put this in the context of a marriage. Your mate did not grow up in a home where milk was spilled at mealtime. In fact, in her home, when a child spilled milk, the child was punished and removed from the table. The first time you spill your milk, your wife's reaction may or may not register on the Richter scale, but after the first month of marriage, thirty spills later, she will have a few choice words to share with you. You can't understand why such a little thing like this can elicit such a huge reaction from her. In fact, you are convinced that she has gone over the edge, and you can't imagine why she rails at you, attacks your character, and insists that you are making her life miserable at every meal *on purpose*.

Whose perspective is right? Although this scenario is a bit exaggerated, it is much like what I see happening in marriages every day. One person behaves repeatedly in a certain way with no idea that the behavior is a product of history. He or she marries someone with a dissimilar history, and the fireworks begin. Many couples spend a great deal of time either defending their histories ("I've always done it this way, and I'm not about to change now") or trying to change their mates ("Your method of washing the car is ridiculous! Can't you see that my way is the way it should be done?").

Hence, looking at your history is vital to building a strong marriage because:

1. You carry your history with you. It plays itself out in your daily life, affecting your thoughts, feelings, behaviors, and thus your relationships. Awareness opens the door for future change.

2. Your history is a rich source for understanding your mate and yourself. Much conflict can be resolved with greater understanding.

3. Your history is the baseline from which God transforms you. God views spiritual transformation as a tremendous benefit.

4. God encourages you to "remember the days of old, consider the generations long past" (Deuteronomy 32:7). Remembering is a means of reflecting on God's

faithfulness in your life, as well as a source of adora-
tion to God for His work of transformation.

Throughout this book, we will come back to these four principles. They will be building blocks for the foundation of a
stronger relationship. If you will allow God access, He will bring
about restoration that you may not know you need. The apostle
Paul declares in his letter to the Ephesians, "God can do anything, you know — far more than you could ever imagine or guess
or request in your wildest dreams! He does it not by pushing us
around but by working within us, his Spirit deeply and gently
within us" (Ephesians 3:20, MSG).

We have shared these principles with many who have under-
taken the hard work of restoration and watched as God gave them
back a better relationship than what they thought possible. *The
Message* puts it this way:

> *These words I speak to you are not incidental additions to
> your life, homeowner improvements to your standard of living.
> They are foundational words*, words to build a life on. *If you
> work these words into your life, you are like a smart carpenter
> who built his house on solid rock. Rain poured down, the river
> flooded, a tornado hit — but nothing moved that house. It was
> fixed to the rock.* (Matthew 7:24-25, emphasis added)

"Foundational words, words to build a life on." Meditate on
that for a moment. You may hesitate to begin this journey
because you may not know where it may lead you. Right now,
before we go any further, pause and pray. Be honest with God
about what you're feeling. This prayer may reflect your heart:

Lord, I'm not sure where this journey is leading me, and I'm not sure I want to be on it. But I do want to be open to all that You have for me. I want a strong, loving relationship with my mate that lasts and brings honor to You. If exploring my history is a part of this process, then I want to give You complete access, fully believing that you are a God who redeems and restores. Help me now to hold nothing back, but to surrender to you all that I was, all that I am, and all that I can become by Your grace. In Jesus' name, amen.

If you have prayed this or a similar prayer, know that God is faithful to do that which you cannot do on your own. Your part is to trust Him and to follow.

The journey begins now.

ACTION STEP: REFLECT ON PATTERNS

Take a few minutes with a pen and paper and record some of the relational patterns you have carried with you. If you have trouble coming up with patterns, it may help to think about some of the conflicts you and your spouse have had. Don't just look at the subject of the conflicts, but look at your style differences in dealing with the conflicts. If you have trouble identifying areas, chapter 2 may help you.

HISTORY IN THE MAKING

"PAY ATTENTION — THIS IS HISTORY IN THE MAKING!" DO
you remember one of your parents saying this to you about
an event during your childhood? Most of us can recall certain
momentous occasions that stand out as we reflect on the past.

Some historical events are monumental in my mind. Most in
my generation remember exactly where they were when they
heard the news of President John F. Kennedy's assassination. My
husband vividly remembers the events at Kent State and the war
in Viet Nam, as he was subject to the draft. We remember Ed
Sullivan introducing the Beatles on his "really big shew," astro-
nauts landing on the moon, and the flower children of the late six-
ties. Likewise, my children's memories of September 11, 2001, will
be something they will recall to their children and grandchildren.

We all experience history in the making — and we are all prod-
ucts of our histories. Yet most of us live our lives obliquely.
Growing up in our families, we rarely ponder the effect our sur-
roundings will have on us one day. The "everydayness" of our lives
rarely ranks with the momentous world events we remember. But
our histories are important.

In this chapter, we're going to explore three types of historical baggage that we carry into our marriages. There are *treasured*

traits — positive qualities developed within our families and other significant relationships. *Tarnished traditions* are the repetitive patterns, expectations, and predispositions we have adopted from our histories. And *tabled transgressions* are the obvious and obscure losses we've all experienced but haven't considered significant in our present or future.

TREASURED TRAITS

I ran into my friend Mae's in-laws recently in the parking lot of the nearby grocery store. Now in their eighties, Ray and Thelma are still vibrant and excited about life, even though both have had serious health problems. I've had the pleasure of observing them with their family over the last twenty years, and what a privilege they have been to watch! After inquiring about their health, I told them how blessed I'd been by their godly influence and involvement in their adult children's lives and families. I related how much I admired them for their respectful approach — always available, but never intrusive. Both of them blushed a bit and then Ray said, "We only passed on what we both had from our parents. We were blessed with godly parents who taught us about prayer, hard work, and loving the Lord. We're so grateful to the Lord for our heritage." I hugged them both and told them that their legacy would not remain with their children alone. I too had benefited from their winsome ways. I said, "I hope that I can be the type of grandparent someday that you have so excellently modeled."

As I got into my car and waved good-bye that afternoon, I couldn't help but have tears in my eyes. I was both sorrowful and joyful. Sorrowful, because I longed to have a conversation with my own godly grandmother who died when I was twenty-four.

Joyful, as I thought of my stepgrandfather, whose love for God and the Scripture had made a tremendous impact on my life, even though our contact was limited during my growing-up years. My grandpa Ray died when I was nineteen — how I have yearned for his words of wisdom and counsel over the years!

Think for a moment about growing up in your home. What are some of the things you value most? Who significantly influenced your life for the good? What character qualities do you possess that reflect that person's influence in your life? How have you been diligent in feeding into your children the same nourishment you received?

No matter what your history, there are positive things to be gleaned that you must intentionally preserve and pass on. Take a few moments and jot down some specific traits or behavior patterns displayed in your immediate family, extended family, or other relationships that produced good fruit in your life. It is never too late to be thankful for those things and to ask God to help you reproduce a similar harvest in your own family and relationships.

TARNISHED TRADITIONS

Unfortunately, just as some of the positive traits become second nature to us, so do some of the negative ones.

For instance, all of us bring with us certain repetitive patterns, expectations, and predispositions that can radically affect not only how we view marriage, but also how we participate in it.

I think of Nancy and Scott. Nancy grew up with little supervision from her alcoholic mother, who divorced her father when Nancy was five. Nancy was in charge since she was seven years old. She took care of her two younger siblings and made sure the house was in order so her mother did not have that burden. As a result of being overly responsible her whole life, she was desperately looking for someone to take care of her when she married. She wanted a capable, strong man who had his ducks in a row. Scott fit the bill. Scott was a successful businessman who had built his company from the ground up. He was extremely efficient and hardworking. Scott's father had immigrated to this country and worked two jobs to make ends meet. Although Scott had worked with his father in the family business, Scott never seemed to measure up to his father's perfectionist standards. When Scott married, he had definite ideas about where he wanted to be financially by the time he retired, and as a result, he had little time to invest in Nancy or their three children.

When they came in for counseling, both Nancy and Scott were very disillusioned with each other. All Nancy wanted was a husband who would "be there" for her and the kids. Instead, she had a lovely home, financial security, and a husband who didn't seem to notice she needed him. All Scott wanted was a wife who appreciated the sacrifices he'd made to provide such a wonderful living for his family and recognition for his accomplishments.

Both Nancy and Scott neglected to look at their histories as significantly influencing their relationship and expectations of each other. They didn't realize how each of them brought hidden expectations that were direct correlates of their experiences in childhood. They were able to report the history of their families without ever identifying how the experiences in their homes were shaping their marriage. It was through surveying their families of origin, noting the observable truth, and then examining how those events affected their own needs, views, and expectations of their mates that they were able to change and develop more satisfying ways of relating to one another. "What intrigues me, always," writes Dr. Maggie Scarf in her book *Intimate Partners*, "is the way in which two individuals—who often have emerged from families with very different sets of rules for interacting, behaving, and even *thinking* about life—come together to hammer out a new system of their own devising."[1]

TABLED TRANSGRESSIONS

Our tarnished ways of thinking and acting are usually responses to experiences we've had in the past. I call those experiences "tabled transgressions" because they often involve ways in which imperfect people have transgressed against us, and we often have tabled or hidden them from view. You may already know what your significant experiences were, but you don't know what to do with what you've discovered. Or you may not know how to begin identifying the key experiences of your past. The following analogy may help you survey your history.

Your life might be compared to a business. In the business world, corporations hire an accountant to prepare what is called a profit and loss statement. This statement is a summary that itemizes the company's income and expenses. Its purpose is to show whether or not the corporation is profitable. In addition to the "P & L," as it is referred to, a balance sheet is also prepared. The balance sheet lists the corporation's assets and liabilities. The assets of a company include all that is *owned*—any monies in bank accounts, purchased equipment, such as a desk or computer, or any other assets the corporation has acquired. The liabilities of a company include all that is *owed*—any debts, loans, or investment capital that has been lent to the corporation. The corporation is the sum total of its income and expenses and its assets and liabilities. In other words, these things *are* the corporation, not its purpose or function.

Imagine you own a pizza parlor. Your pizza business is made up of your income and expenses each month, in combination with your assets and liabilities. Your business purpose as a pizza parlor is to provide pizza to your customers. Your ability to function as a pizza parlor providing pizza to your customers depends upon the consolidation of what you own and what you owe.

Our lives are like the corporation. We are a consolidation of what we own and what we owe: the profitable assets carried into our adult life that build and benefit us, and the liabilities and indebtedness that burden and block us from our potential of "profitability."

In this book we are focusing mostly on the "liabilities and indebtedness" we each bring to our relationships. We might more simply refer to these as the "losses" that have resulted from living in a sinful world. Like the corporation, we must be aware of our losses and liabilities, but it is sometimes painful to face the realities of loss. I remember how difficult it was after our flood going from room to room, looking at what had been damaged and lost. It was overwhelming, but necessary.

As marriage partners, we must survey our individual losses before we can intelligently build a joint relationship. We sometimes neglect this vital step because we tend to minimize or table our losses, unaware of their significance. Most of us don't experience a fire or flood that completely devastates our home. But we do experience some type of loss as a result of living in a less-than-perfect world with less-than-perfect people. We may have a closet full of ridicule that was heaped on by an overbearing relative, a cabinet stuffed with resentment from a previous marriage, or a cupboard full of disappointment over a parent who seldom kept his promises. We may have a corner of heartache in the basement because we never reached our potential in sports, or an attic full of resentment toward a sibling who was the favored child. If we aren't honest about these losses and don't seek God for the necessary restoration, we will often inadvertently replicate the patterns with those closest to us, or we will guard our hearts and close ourselves off from those who have the potential to hurt us again.

SURVEYING YOUR LOSSES

The book of Nehemiah gives us a wonderful biblical illustration of the necessity to survey the losses before we start the rebuilding process. Nehemiah was a godly man who had a burden to rebuild the wall around Jerusalem, a wall that had been devastated by the enemy. The Scripture tells us that after months of prayer and preparation, Nehemiah received permission from the king to leave his job in Persia and travel to Jerusalem to complete the project. The first thing he did when he arrived was survey the damage. He went all around at night "examining the walls of Jerusalem, which had been broken down, and its gates, which had been destroyed by fire" (Nehemiah 2:13).

This principle is so crucial! We must survey the damage before we can rebuild. I've known couples who have tried to build on faulty foundations, only to have their marriages crumble. But Nehemiah told his fellow workers the truth about their condition: "You see the trouble we are in: Jerusalem lies in ruins, and its gates have been burned with fire. Come, let us rebuild the wall of Jerusalem, and we will no longer be in disgrace" (Nehemiah 2:17).

Nehemiah didn't pretend! He assessed the situation accurately and determined a course of action that resulted in a remedy.

We will return to this example later, but for now, the significant point is that he surveyed the situation before trying to rectify it.

I truly believe that the failure of many Christians to assess and address these losses accurately has resulted in the downfall of many marriages. We are painfully aware that the divorce rates do not vary significantly between nonChristians and those who claim to follow Christ. We're told that "sin" is the culprit, but I wonder if that generalization is not an oversimplification. Many relationships end because wounded hearts and sinful patterns carried into the marriage are not assessed and addressed.

In contrast, I have seen many couples headed toward divorce who have taken seriously their need to look at their issues and work through them — and whose marriages have been restored. I have also helped couples with good marriages implement the surveying of loss and develop a deeper intimacy and commitment because they understood each other more fully than before.

Why does it work for some and not for others? Sometimes couples or individuals are in denial, refusing to look honestly at themselves to avoid emotional pain. Other times they are genuinely unaware that such patterns exist and have the capacity to destroy a relationship. Too often, couples fall victim to discouragement, laziness, or apathy. They think there is "little hope for change," "there's too much work to do," and "it takes too much time." They fall into passive resignation, which is deadly in all relationships.

You may be reading this clearly knowing what background issues (losses, liabilities) you have brought into your marriage. You may have been abused, your previous spouse may have been unfaithful, your parents may have divorced, you may have grown up in a rigid religious system, your father may have been a workaholic, or your mother may have been emotionally unavailable. Or, you may not see any connection between your history and your present marriage. You may even have detailed opinions about how your partner's history is affecting your marriage but no idea of how your own history fits in.

I have found it helpful to explore my history similarly to the way in which Nehemiah approached the wall repair in Jerusalem. He surveyed it thoroughly, wept over the loss and destruction, and set about to rebuild it with the "gracious hand of God upon him."

In order to survey your history, it may help to consider two different types of loss or brokenness most of us experience. There are *obvious losses*, which are readily apparent as we survey our life, and there are *obscure losses*, which are less evident.

OBVIOUS LOSSES

A counselor friend shared this metaphor with me several years ago: Imagine your life as a desert flatland at sunset. As you look across the expansive horizon, you see several things that stand out. There are mountains, hills, boulders, cacti, and brambly tumbleweeds. All of these are stationed prominently against the backdrop of the horizon. They represent "acts of commission"—things that happen to you, around you, or against you. They are things such as divorce, abandonment, alcoholism, abuse, perfectionism, infidelity, cruelty, pornography exposure, and favoritism. These "committed acts" injured and shaped you even when the people involved did not set out to harm you. Family members and others made poor choices for themselves that had ripple effects in your life. These acts were results of sin and selfishness that plague all human beings. Most of the time you can identify acts of commission because they are so

obvious when you view the horizon of your life. But you may minimize or suppress the impact of such acts of commission because
"it was just what happened"—it was life.

These obvious losses, if not attended to, will continue to
wreak havoc in your personal life and relationships. They are at
the root of many bitter divorces and the crux of intact marriages
that remain lifeless.

My friend Brad told me of one such oversight in his years in
the restoration business. He was called out to do a final inspection
on a home damaged by fire. The restoration company had spent
several months on the project and was in the final stages of
painting before what is called the "occupancy" stage: once the
final inspection is complete, the family is allowed to reoccupy the
dwelling. Brad toured the home, and everything on the surface
looked good. Before completing his walk-through, he noticed an
attic access in one of the closets and climbed up to inspect. He was
shocked by what he found. The entire attic area within view was
cremated. The electrical wiring was charred but not burned
through, so the circuitry still operated. After further investigation,
he discovered that the workers had indeed repaired a portion of
the attic area, visible through a hallway access, but they neglected
to see this damage. His years of experience helped him conduct a
thorough survey. The damaged area of the attic was directly above
the kitchen, and had the discovery not been made, the ceiling
most likely would have caved in or another fire would have
resulted. Brad said it was extremely fortunate for the company
that the discovery was made, although it was a costly oversight.

As in this case, so it is in some relationships—you may need
the assistance of someone with experience and a trained eye to
help you survey the damage that you might otherwise overlook.

Not every couple needs a counselor, but no one should feel embarrassed to seek assistance.

Obvious losses or "acts of commission" are often results of sinful repetitive patterns that have been adopted from previous generations. That is why doing this work is so important. In order to leave a legacy of integrity, honesty, and godliness with our children, we must examine our own lives and allow God's Spirit to transform us from the inside out. We will never leave a flawless legacy, but we can leave our children a legacy of faith that God is able and willing to conform us into the image of His Son. Paul exhorted Timothy about how to leave a legacy of faith: "Be diligent in these matters; give yourself wholly to them, so that everyone may see your *progress*. Watch your life and doctrine closely. Persevere in them, because if you do, you will save both yourself and your hearers" (1 Timothy 4:15-16, emphasis added).

OBSCURE LOSSES

Besides obvious losses that stand out prominently in your life, there are obscure losses that are far subtler but just as influential.

Picture again the desert flatland. This time, however, you are not surveying from a distance but are standing in the middle of the desert, looking down at the ground around your feet.

You see dry, parched soil riddled with deep crevices where the land has split, forming gaping holes. There are small cracks that spider web out and form large cracks. As you look wider, you see that the large cracks form gullies and ridges, and the dusty sand looks as though it has not had a drink in years. There may even be vast canyons, eroded over time, which are not visible until you are at the cliff's edge looking down. These deep crevices, cracks, and dry soil represent "acts of omission" — things that are left out, undone, or neglected. Omitted acts may be appropriate love from a parent, bonding (also known as attachment), belonging, security, protection, discipline, nurturing, fueling of self-worth, proper nourishment, positive gender role modeling, guidance, safety, and consistency. These acts of omission or neglect are just as powerful as acts of commission, but they are overlooked because they are not obvious as you survey the landscape of your life.

I was reminded of this several years ago after an earthquake. A major earthquake centered about twenty-five miles from our home in California in October 1987. It hit the city of Whittier very hard, and several buildings were demolished. The morning it hit, my two daughters and I were sitting at the dining table eating breakfast when the rumble began. The oak hutch with my china and crystal in it started rattling. Heather and Kellie screamed, and we ran to a doorway between our living room and den. Huddled there together, we prayed out loud. What started out as a shaking turned into a series of minor jolts. It seemed to last forever and I was alarmed. Finally it stopped—but would another more serious one follow? We learned from the television that it was a big one—a 5.9 magnitude. I inspected the damage in our home and nothing was broken, but several pieces of my china overturned and six crystal goblets lay pressed against the glass doors of my china cabinet. It wasn't until several months later that I discovered a thin crack from ceiling to floor behind our living room drapes.

Sometimes earthquake damage is not visible to the eye, and that is what makes it dangerous. A contractor friend of ours told us of such an occurrence after the Whittier quake. He was called out to a Whittier home to conduct an inspection. The family continued living in their home because it appeared to have suffered only minor damage. Then they began noticing oddities.

The doors in their house were not closing properly, a window broke, and the walls seemed to be rising. It was soon discovered that the home had suffered several fractures in its foundation during the quake. The faulty foundation was causing the home to shift and resulted in the abnormalities the homeowners observed. Little did they know that they were in grave danger — the home could have collapsed at any time, without warning.

Sometimes "obscure losses" are like the subtle variations experienced by the homeowners. You may be aware of the loss or omission, or you may not. The losses may be hidden underneath layers of time, but the effects are lived out daily.

It is important to note that acts of omission are, for the most part, an unintentional oversight by those who were responsible to care for us. These omitted things leave us with hairline cracks and gaping wounds that we may try to fill ourselves. Some try to fill them with money, success, prestige, and power. Others try to fill or numb them with food, drugs, alcohol, pornography, or various addictions. Just as with the acts of commission, the injuries of omission must be recognized and dealt with in order for us to grow in healthy patterns of relating.

ACTION STEP: ROADMAP YOUR HISTORY

Take a moment and survey your life. It might be helpful to sit down with a large piece of paper and make a road map. Start the map from your birth. Draw a line (it can be straight, curved, or with twists and turns) and landmarks that indicate significant events in your history. Include whatever stands out prominently in your mind as pivotal or important. The events may not be tragic or momentous, but they register with you as a vital link in your history. Some "events" are really ongoing conditions, such as living with a chronically ill parent. Continue your map to the present.

Next, on a separate piece of paper, write a few sentences about each landmark that tell how you felt about that event at the time and how you feel about it now.

Third, review your road map, asking yourself what you were missing at the different stages of your life. Indicate these omissions on your road map by V-shaped lines in which you place a word or phrase that describes what you needed. Afterward, write a short paragraph about these losses, describing how you feel about them now. Ideally, you and your mate should do this exercise independently and then share your road maps with each other.

The following page provides an example of what a road map might look like. Pray and ask God to shed His light on your life and show you how He wants to meet you on that map. He is not a God who is subject to time and space as we know it. He is a God who transcends time and can heal any hurt, bind up any broken heart, and set every captive free.

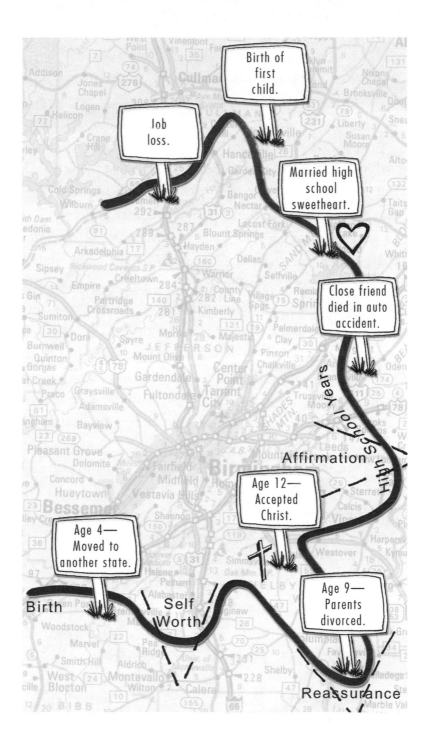

CLAIMING YOUR HISTORY

Now that you're aware of the three types of historical baggage and you've surveyed your life with your road map, what do you do next?

We have a simple formula that may help you understand how to deal with your history. You face it, trace it, erase it, and replace it. You must first *face* the negative patterns you have from your history, then *trace* them back to their roots, take steps to *erase* them, and *replace* them with healthier patterns. We discovered how important this process was early in our marriage through something as routine as mealtimes.

I noticed a pattern at dinner. After spending over an hour preparing a lovely dinner, all four of us gathered at the table, filled our plates, and began eating. Our young daughters tried to initiate conversation while Don and I inhaled our food. We nodded and grunted occasionally with our mouths full, but we finished our meal within five minutes flat. I realized we were not utilizing our mealtime as a time of connection. I asked Don, "I wonder why we do this? Why do we come to the table, eat as fast as we can, and take so little time to enjoy each other?"

Don replied without hesitation, "Honey, in my family there were seven kids. You had to eat fast to get your fair share!" Don humorously called this defensive eating. When he said this, I immediately thought back to my history. We ate promptly at 5:30 every evening. My mother prepared very nice meals, but my stepfather's demeanor at the table was less than pleasant. He spent most of the time criticizing us and speaking in a derogatory tone to my mother. I developed the art of fast eating so I could be excused from the table.

Don and I faced a pattern, traced it back to its roots, and

decided we wanted to do dinnertime differently. We felt it important to create a warm and inviting atmosphere around the table, and we discussed how we might encourage dialogue. Heather was four and Kellie was two at the time. Don employed Heather's help in designing and decorating a "question box." He and Heather took an old shoebox, decorated it with magazine clippings of fun activities, and cut a slit in the top. Each family member placed questions in the box throughout the week (with the assistance of a parent's writing skills), and after dinner we each picked out a slip from the box and answered the question. At the time, our girls' questions were typical of their age, such as: "Why is the sky blue?" or "Who on Sesame Street do you like the best: Bert, Ernie, or the Cookie Monster?" Don and I used it as a great communication tool, asking questions like: "If you could choose your dream vacation, where would you go?" or "What would be an ideal date night?"

We used the "question box" for years, making age-appropriate adjustments. When the girls reached elementary school, we bought placemats of the United States. Don, who loves history and geography, would ask the girls questions about places on the map, and we'd share stories about places we'd been. We changed a pattern from our history and have reaped beneficial results. Not all patterns from history are this easily remedied, but you can use this simple concept as you approach your own history.

We'll start with facing your history and learning from it. What does it mean to learn from your history? My husband, who has been in education for more than thirty years, defines learning this way: It is a change in behavior as a result of experience. It is not enough to know about your history; that knowing needs to be applied in an understanding way. God calls this *wisdom*. By examining your history and using the information to initiate change, you are on your way to a stronger marriage.

CHAPTER 3

LEARNING FROM YOUR HISTORY

FACING

JIM AND MARY SAT CLOSE TOGETHER ON THE SOFA IN MY office, holding hands. They were both in their mid-thirties, eagerly anticipating their marriage in four months. I learned they had recently completed a six-week marriage preparation class at their church and were interested in follow-up counseling. They took a relationship assessment test that indicated they needed help in the areas of communication and conflict resolution. I asked them about their histories.

Mary was divorced with no children. She described her first husband as controlling and verbally abusive. She commented that she tended to be in relationships that were emotionally abusive.

"Mary, tell me about your family growing up," I asked.

"I have three older brothers, and my mom and dad have been married forty-six years."

"Tell me about your relationship with your parents," I urged.

"My mother is out in left field. We don't have much of a relationship. She's very controlling, and I don't know how my dad has put up with it all these years. My dad is pretty distant. He worked a lot while I was growing up, and drank a lot."

"If you could use a word to describe your parents' marriage, what would that word be?"

"Disgruntled. That's the first word that comes to my mind."

I turned to Jim and asked him to tell me a little about himself. Jim had never been married. His mother and father divorced when he was in his twenties, and his mother owned and ran the company where he was presently employed. He had two sisters, one of whom also worked in the family business.

"How would you describe your parents' marriage prior to their divorce?" I asked.

"Unpredictable," Jim said. "There were definitely times of closeness, but much more I remember them fighting."

"It sounds like neither of you had a very good model of marriage in your home growing up," I observed.

I spent the remainder of the session talking about how I might help them as a couple improve their communication and learn some healthy conflict resolution techniques.

"But," I added, "one of the things that will be extremely important is for us to look together at both of your histories." We discussed the importance of exploring Mary's previous marriage, since that was part of her history that she brought to the relationship. "We will also need to look carefully at your families in several areas, such as communication, conflict, finances, parenting, and how love was communicated in your home."

I explained to Jim and Mary that, even though they were now adults and had left home, many of the patterns they learned in their families and in other relationships were carried with them into their present relationships. They needed to face their histories and the present patterns that existed. I explained that we do not automatically shed the familiar, ingrained styles of relating that we observed and participated in for most of our formative years. We tend to replicate what we have known with little thought or intention, simply because we are doing what comes naturally or is familiar.

I shared the following illustration. My husband, Don, grew up in a large family. There was always enough food to eat and a nice home to live in, but money was not abundant. As a result, Don is frugal and careful with money. On the other hand, I grew up in a middle-class home where appearances were very important. My parents used credit cards, and although my stepdad was in the banking business, I was never taught money management. I learned that if you wanted something you couldn't afford, you charged it. My philosophy was that as long as there were checks in the checkbook, there was money in the bank. Don had trouble with this philosophy when we first married!

Because Don and I had such different backgrounds regarding money, we were destined for conflict. There were plenty of late-night discussions and misunderstandings over how we approached finances and spending. We've spent considerable time in our marriage doing two things: first, understanding and facing our differences; and second, together formulating a workable plan that we could agree on concerning how we would handle finances in our home and what we would teach our children.

By this time, Jim and Mary were getting the point. They acknowledged that neither of them had very good examples of communication or conflict resolution in their homes growing up. And Mary realized she'd had similar problems in her previous marriage. Now they understood why this area had been a sore spot in their relationship. They would need to work together to explore their histories and be willing to make needed adjustments and changes. I assured them that God is bigger than their histories and that, with His help, they could build a strong, satisfying marriage that would last.

You may need to face your history as well. Facing your history simply means that you recognize and deal with it straightforwardly. Most of us grow up in our homes with little need to assess or evaluate. As children, we absorb the definitions of marriage, family, and relationships through experience. We incorporate those meanings into our lives without consideration or examination, and they become the stage for conflict in our own marriages. Maggie Scarf writes,

> Families, all families are intensely emotional social systems
> (even those that appear to contain no emotionality whatsoever). It is within this highly emotional setting that each of us
> learns a particular set of rules, regulations, and expectations
> about our own and other people's behavior that eventually
> become taken for granted as obvious matters that everybody
> knows about.[1]

EVERY HOUSE HAS A HISTORY

In preparation for writing this book, I accompanied my friend Brad to a home that had recently suffered a devastating fire. Nothing could have prepared me for what I saw. As I stepped from the concrete patio slab, through the blown-out sliding glass doorframe, and into the small dinette area, the scene and smell took my breath away. I stood next to the small dinette table with scorched chair cushions neatly tied. Blackened lemons, oranges, and limes sat on the wooden table, recognizable by their shape and a hint of remaining color. The walls in the living room were blackened and the contents of the room were ashes. The hollowed-out staircase leading upstairs reminded me of something out of a creepy movie.

People lived here, I thought to myself. I could barely hear the voice of my guide as he pointed out the various stages of the fire damage in an experienced, matter-of-fact tone. He had assessed many similar sites in his years in the restoration business.

"Do you know what started the fire?" I asked.

He'd heard that the young couple who lived there were newlyweds, married just three months. Apparently, a kitten had knocked over a lit candle in the upstairs bedroom and so started the fire. I couldn't help imagining this young couple. They must have been overcome with grief about the treasured photos of their wedding, the quilt given by a great-grandmother, the linens they'd picked out during their engagement, and the cards and notes they'd saved during courtship to share with their children some day. All of it was gone. They would go on, find another place to live, buy new furniture, and begin to build new memories. However, this event would be a landmark in their lives.

Not all of us have histories with such dramatic landmarks, but some do.

OUR STORY

It may help to share our story. Don and I met on a blind date. I was twenty-two. Don was twenty-seven. I was not walking with the Lord at the time we met, but God was in the process of wooing me back to a more committed life. Don and I dated for six months before I realized that although I cared deeply about Don, I could not continue the relationship.

Don had grown up in a religious home and was truly a man

of integrity, but he was not a Christian. I knew there was no future for us without both of us being committed to Christ, so we went our separate ways. Four months after our breakup, Don made a personal decision for Christ, aided by a man on staff with Campus Crusade for Christ. We stayed in contact with each other, but Don moved out of the area and we pursued different directions. We reunited in the fall of 1978, two years after we met. By the spring of 1979, I was convinced Don was the man I was to marry, but Don was not so sure. We decided to make an appointment to counsel with his pastor.

I am so grateful today for the wise counsel Pastor Mike gave us. "It is clear to me that you both love each other and love the Lord," Pastor Mike said. "I think it would be helpful for you to set aside a specific amount of time for prayer and seeking God's direction. If you believe it is God's will for you to marry, you need to set a date and get on with your life. If not, you need to separate, release each other, and move on with your individual lives." He then looked at Don and said, "Don, you're not getting any younger (Don was thirty), and I think part of what is holding you back is the emotional tie that remains with your family."

Pastor Mike didn't know my history, or he would have turned to me with a similar observation about my family entanglement. After leaving the office that day, Don decided he needed a month to pray. I'm thankful it didn't take that long! In fact, Don showed up at my workplace five days later and proposed. We set a date and were married in October of 1979, three years after we met. We were both sure by this time that God truly was calling us together, and we were ready to make a lifetime commitment.

We thought we knew each other well because we had discussed our backgrounds and what we wanted in a mate. What we didn't know was that our backgrounds were still very much a part of our lives. Pastor Mike's words foreshadowed what we would experience in the early years of marriage.

DON'S STORY

I (Don) was the oldest boy in a family of seven children. I still remember the first time I saw my father. I was five years old and I remember seeing my dad in his navy dress uniform returning from the Korean War. I have no idea how his experience of war affected the man I grew up with. Nobody talked about such things. All I know is that from my earliest memory, he had a relationship with alcohol. It wasn't so bad in my early years, but through setbacks in my father's military career and other difficult circumstances, his drinking progressed to the point of severe alcoholism.

My Scandinavian/German heritage contributed to the family's sense of deep loyalty and restricted emotion. Most of the time growing up, my father's alcoholism was denied or ignored. My mother did her best to raise us children and keep the family afloat.

By the time Jan and I met and were dating, my father's alcoholism was severe enough to warrant hospitalization and detoxification. Jan worked in a probation department when we met and had attended several training sessions on alcoholism. She realized that my family showed classic signs of an alcoholic's legacy. My mother had difficulty finding the strength to deal with or confront my father's behavior. We children, now adults, struggled with many of the common symptoms of growing up in an alcoholic home: Don't talk, don't trust, and don't feel.[2] These unspoken rules of the alcoholic/dysfunctional family permeated the air, but we were in denial about the problem. We had ingested these rules into our lives without awareness, as though we were breathing in toxins from the atmosphere.

One practical way in which this legacy affected our marriage was my intense need to avoid conflict. Having watched my parents fight over my father's drinking for many years and never resolve the problem, I automatically pretended that all was well between Jan and me, whether it was or not. Without consciously thinking the matter through, I had drawn the conclusion that conflict was painful and solved nothing. My motto was *leave it alone and it may get better on its own or just go away.* Until I faced this belief and traced it to its source in my history, Jan and I stumbled over conflict repeatedly.

Further, when we first married I had a tough time sharing my feelings because I didn't know I had any. In my family I learned that any smart person would push his feelings to the side in order to survive pain and disappointment. One day I came home from work and told Jan about an interaction I'd had with a coworker. She said, "It's no wonder you're angry about that." I immediately replied, "I'm not angry." I wasn't aware of feeling angry, and it bothered me to be accused of something I didn't feel. Jan said, "Honey, I think you are angry because you're red in the face and the veins are popping out in your neck." I snapped, "I am NOT angry and I resent you telling me that I am!"

Finally, one of my greatest challenges has been to overcome anxiety in situations that I can't control. Because I grew up in a home that was unpredictable and out of control, I hate feeling out of control. As a boy I learned to busy myself when things felt shaky at home. Not far into our marriage, I realized that I would go into "performance mode" anytime I thought Jan was upset with me over something. I wouldn't ask her about it or try to work it out (that never worked in my family); I would simply iron my clothes, clean up the garage, finish a project, or do the dishes to try to get back into Jan's good graces. You may be thinking, *I wish my mate would do that—we might get some things done around here!* But trust me, it wasn't good for either my wife or myself.

Even though Jan and I had information about how growing up in an alcoholic home affects people, we were convinced that because I was a Christian, those effects would be only minimal for us. We couldn't have been more wrong.

JAN'S STORY

My history was no less damaging. I was the youngest of three girls, and my parents divorced when I was five. Two years after the divorce, my oldest sister married and moved out. That left my sister Kathy, who is four years older, and me at home. My mother worked full time to support us, and she eventually married my stepfather when I was eight years old. She had grown up in a Christian home but had fallen away from her early faith. My stepfather also had grown up in a Christian home and, after marrying my mother, insisted we attend a Bible-believing church in our area. It was through the ministry of this church, in an evening service January 17, 1965, that I asked Jesus into my heart to be my personal Lord and Savior.

Three weeks later, while my mother and sister were at a mother-daughter tea at church, my stepfather called me out of my bedroom under the pretense of watching television, and he proceeded to sexually abuse me. A month after this incident, my mother asked if anything had happened. I didn't know at the time that my stepfather was also abusing my older sister. Kathy had told my mom what was going on, and this prompted my mother's question. I told my mom what had happened but never heard another word about it. Life went on. We continued sitting in the pew Sunday after Sunday, looking like the normal Christian family. The abuse continued for both my sister and me until we moved out of the home, although neither of us knew about each other's abuse until we became adults. I discovered later that both my mother and stepfather had sexual abuse in their history that had not been faced.

Like many survivors of abuse, I buried the events of my past and carried on with life. I became an overachiever, trying desperately to cover up the deep insecurity that I felt inside. I went through a rebellious period with the Lord in my late adolescence until I started attending a wonderfully Bible-based fellowship. I then grew in my knowledge of God's Word and recommitted my life to Christ at twenty-two. Eventually I went to my stepfather, told him I forgave him for all that he had done, and was met with stoic denial. He said, "I don't know what you're talking about, but if you need to forgive me — okay." I thought at the time that this chapter of my life was over. I had done everything I needed to do.

It wasn't until about two years into my marriage that the emotional storm that had been brewing in my life began to break loose. Although I had tried to bury my past, it was resurrecting itself in my daily life. My history had crept into my life like a cat burglar robbing me of my most treasured possessions. God used distinct symptoms to show me that my past had not been healed: weekly migraine headaches, depression, anger, jealousy, and a critical attitude toward Don. It wasn't as though my life was a wreck. I taught a Bible study at our church. I had a wonderful Christian husband and a healthy daughter. But I could not deny my internal world of turmoil and the outward manifestations it was producing.

I had to face that I had trust and self-esteem issues that showed up in our day-to-day relationship. If Don spoke of a secretary at work, I was suspicious that he might be wishing he'd married her rather than me. I had difficulty believing Don truly loved me.

Our physical relationship was troubled as well. Because I had been deeply hurt in this area, it was not a simple obstacle to overcome. It took understanding and compassion on both our parts. Don educated himself about abuse and gained insight into the dynamics of families in which this occurs. He used that knowledge to walk with me through the months of counseling and recovery, even though he felt ill-equipped to fully understand or respond to my need for safety.

God made it clear to me that He wanted to heal me, but His healing involved a process of time. Don committed himself to me, sometimes at great personal sacrifice. I didn't know all of what God had in store for me — He didn't provide a road map for the next five years. But He did provide us the grace to walk that next step together. I know God was honoring the prayer of a young wife and mother who desperately wanted to love her husband, love her child, and most important, love her God. That was the beginning of my own journey of healing from the "firestorms" that had ravaged my life. I have detailed that process in my book Door of Hope.[3] My purpose here is not to go into the specifics of my recovery, but only to stress the importance of dealing with our past.

Several years into our marriage, Don faced a similar turning point as he recognized the need to face the effects of his father's alcoholism in his own life.

Both Don and I had to face that the abuse and alcoholism in our backgrounds were affecting us in the present. We both had control issues, unresolved hurt and anger, and unhealthy communication patterns. As a result, we overreacted to many situations and found we were unable to successfully resolve issues. Fortunately, God stepped in to show us that our history and its effects were not beyond His ability to redeem. As we committed ourselves to Him and the process we're sharing in this book, our love for God and each other grew stronger.

YOUR STORY

Facing your history involves recognizing what happened and the effects those experiences have had on the way you relate to people today. How do you face the effects of your history? It is helpful to take an inventory. One trouble I see among couples who come to me for counseling is that they know the facts of what happened, but they don't recognize the patterns that have resulted. How often I hear statements such as, "My mother was a perfectionist," "My father had a drinking problem," or "My brother terrorized me while my parents were out saving souls." The persons who report such facts often cannot see their own critical perfectionism, the way their social drinking is hurting their families, or the hyper-vigilance that was a reasonable response to terror but is now causing problems. Charles Sell wrote, "Facing the facts is not betraying your family. Truth is the issue, not love or loyalty. Love covers a multitude of sins, but it should not distort them. Our objective is not to find fault, but to find help."[4]

Below is an assessment tool to help you identify some of the areas you may want to explore. Before you take the assessment, it may be helpful to note briefly some of the warning signs that indicate "baggage" in a marriage.

BAGGAGE INDICATORS

- *Overreaction to a situation* — The emotional reaction is
  beyond what the situation warrants. (Your spouse forgets to mail the bills and you are enraged.)
- *Repetitive relational patterns that cause conflict with others* —
  Habitual patterns that you employ. (You walk out of the
  room whenever there is tension.)
- *Reenacted patterns of behavior without purposeful intent* —
  Behaviors or reactions that are automatic. ("I explode
  because my dad always did when my parents
  argued.")
- *Heightened sensitivity* — Certain issues are loaded before
  there is any conflict. (You are overly defensive or suspicious about money.)
- *Repeated failure to resolve an issue* — You and your mate
  cannot seem to talk through certain issues with mutual
  successful resolution.
- *Predetermined expectations* — You and/or your mate put
  each other in a box. (You predict his/her negative
  response in advance.)

God's plan for restoration requires a first step of facing reality. For some, this step is monumental because it requires self-
examination coupled with truthful observation. Although the
Bible is clear about our need to examine ourselves (1 Corinthians
11:28; Matthew 7:3-5), many Christians are reluctant to do so. I
am not advocating a posture of self-examination that renders us
paralyzed or stuck in the "blame game." Rather, I encourage an
honest inventory that "guide[s] you into all truth" (John 16:13). We
start this process by invoking the Holy Spirit's help in searching

our hearts. David's simple prayer in Psalm 139 is a great place to start. Pray this prayer before you take the assessment.

> *Investigate my life, O God, find out everything about me;*
> *Cross-examine and test me, get a clear picture of what I'm*
> *about; See for yourself whether I've done anything wrong—*
> *then lead me on the road to eternal life. (Psalm 139:23-24,*
> MSG)

ASSESSMENT TOOL

Answer the following questions, considering what is characteristic of you most of the time. Circle *Y* if the question is true most of the time. Circle *N* if the question is false or not true most of the time.

1. Y N Do you avoid conflict by withdrawing?

2. Y N When your mate offers you suggestions, do you become defensive?

3. Y N When your mate disappoints or hurts you, is it hard to let go of the hurt you feel?

4. Y N Do you expect your mate to be unfaithful at some point in time?

5. Y N Are you jealous of your mate's hobbies, friends, or time apart from you?

6. Y N Despite his or her efforts, do you have trouble believing your mate truly loves you?

7. Y N Do you guard your heart against hurt in your marriage?

8. Y N Do you keep your deep needs and feelings to yourself rather than sharing them with your mate?

9. Y N   When your mate is vulnerable with you about himself or herself, do you use that information during an argument?

10. Y N   Do you expect your mate to "never" change in certain areas?

11. Y N   When you and your mate are having a conflict, do you blow up and leave the room?

12. Y N   Do you use sarcasm to get your point across?

13. Y N   When your mate needs time to himself or herself, do you feel threatened or unloved?

14. Y N   When your mate asks for a need to be met, do you refuse to meet it because you think he/she is trying to control you?

15. Y N   Do you tell partial truths to avoid your mate's displeasure or disappointment?

16. Y N   Do you threaten to leave or divorce when you have an argument?

17. Y N   Do you frequently fantasize about connecting (physically or con-versationally) with a particular person of the opposite sex?

18. Y N   Do you drop hints to get your needs met rather than ask directly?

19. Y N   Do you mentally rehearse past incidents when your mate has hurt you?

20. Y N   When you and your mate have a disagreement, do you keep track of who wins and who loses?

21. Y N   When your mate has a strong opinion, do you have difficulty voicing a different opinion?

22. Y N   Do you get more fulfillment from your job/career than from your marriage?

23. Y N   Do you look for reasons to go to the office?

24. Y N   Do you use humor to mask how you really feel?

25. Y N   When you and your mate go out for an evening, do you often end up in conflict?

26. Y N   Do you find yourself avoiding time alone with your mate?

27. Y N   Do you think your mate is responsible for your happiness?

28. Y N Do you look primarily to your sexual relationship to provide the closeness you need?

29. Y N Do you have trouble saying, "I was wrong. I'm sorry. Please forgive me"?

30. Y N Do you remind your mate of his/her past mistakes?

31. Y N Do you think conflicts are a sign of a "troubled" marriage?

32. Y N Do you regularly have to adjust your schedule to make time for your mate?

33. Y N Do you confide more in a friend or coworker than in your mate?

34. Y N Do you and your mate tend to have conflict over the same issues *repeatedly* without satisfactory resolution?

35. Y N Do you think your mate should know what you are thinking in certain situations without your expressing your thoughts?

36. Y N Do you feel guilty when you're angry?

37. Y N Do you have sex with your mate more out of obligation than desire?

38. Y N When decisions need to be made, do you frequently say to your mate, "Whatever you want is fine"?

39. Y N When having sex with your mate, are you absent emotionally?

40. Y N Do you agree with your mate so as to avoid conflict?

Now that you've taken inventory, let's sort out the answers.

Each question falls into one of the following categories. Circle the number for each question to which you answered yes. If you answered yes to two or more questions in a category, this may be an area of your marriage that needs attention. Some questions/categories may overlap so that issues feed into other areas.

- Communication skills: 2, 12, 18, 24, 25, 35
- Conflict resolution: 1, 9, 11, 16, 29, 34, 40
- Anger/Unforgiveness: 3, 19, 20, 30, 36
- Workaholism: 22, 23, 32

- Intimacy/Closeness: 7, 8, 17, 26, 28, 33, 37, 39
- Expectations: 4, 5, 10, 14, 31
- Self-Esteem/Self-Confidence: 6, 13, 15, 21, 27, 38

The following questions have a strong probability of being "baggage" from your history. Again, circle the number for each question to which you answered yes.

- Baggage: 1, 4, 6, 8, 10, 12, 14, 18,

                             21, 22, 24, 27, 31, 35, 36,

                             37, 39, 40

You may have noticed that there are certain areas of overlap among the questions and categories in the assessment. If you found that your "yes" answers were predominant in a category, that may be the place to begin. You begin by facing your need for growth in this area and committing yourself to pursue change. *The path toward change runs toward truth, not away from it.* We'll discuss in chapter six how to determine whether or not these patterns have their roots in your history and how to respond to them.

We cannot change our histories, but we can learn from them. When you constructed your road map, you recorded significant historical events that have affected you. Now that you've taken your inventory, you have assessed *how* those events along with others affect your present. The next piece of facing your history has to do with understanding a three-dimensional approach to "leaving and cleaving." In some ways it's easier to face the obvious losses of life in an alcoholic home than the obscure effects of leaving home physically but not emotionally. Moving out of your parents' home is not all there is to leaving! And moving in with your spouse is not all there is to becoming "one flesh" with him or her. It took Don and me considerable time to figure this out.

CHAPTER 4

LEAVING YOUR FAMILY OF ORIGIN

BODY, SOUL, AND SPIRIT

MOST OF US ARE FAMILIAR WITH THE SCRIPTURE PASSAGE in Genesis 2:24 regarding marriage because it is so often quoted at weddings and mentioned from the pulpit. We've been taught that the process of marriage includes three distinct phases: leaving, cleaving, and becoming one flesh. We're told that when a man and woman marry they must leave their parents, cleave to their spouse, and so become "one flesh."

There is no doubt that when God first established the foundational principle of "leaving and cleaving," the cultural context was totally foreign to what you and I experience today. But because God's Word can be counted on to transcend time and culture, we should attempt to understand and apply these principles within our modern society. In the simplest of terms, God honors the marriage covenant as supremely important. He tells us that when we marry, we are to "leave" our mother and father. "Leave is the Hebrew word *azab*, which means to loosen, relinquish, forsake, to leave utterly and totally."[1] We are to honor our parents, but we have an even higher obligation to protect and honor our marriage.

What we have seldom been taught is how that "leaving" is to

take place. You may be thinking, "That's easy enough. You pack up your belongings, move out of your parents' home, and move in with your mate."

In counseling many couples over the years, I have found that many have moved out of their parents' homes physically but have not done so in two other areas that are vital to the successful formation and consolidation of their marriage. We are three-dimensional beings made up of body, soul, and spirit. Leaving must take place on all three of these levels if a couple is to bond (cleave) together as God intended. We will speak of these levels as distinct for the purpose of clarity, but they are not independent of one another. The opposite is true. Just as our body, soul, and spirit are interdependent, the process of leaving is interconnected. Leaving is progressive and may occur on all three levels simultaneously. You may not have thought about leaving in this way, but as you will see, it provides a necessary foundation for building a strong marriage.

DRAWN TO THE FAMILIAR

Five years after Don and I married, we were ready to buy our first home. We'd purchased a town home when we married, but with two children it was time to expand our living space. I was very pregnant with our second daughter, Kellie, when our town home sold. We looked frantically for the home that was right for our growing family. We vacillated between two homes. Both had features we liked, but Don seemed to like one better than the other because of the lot size and the overall floor plan. I initially favored the other house, but in the end, we decided on Don's choice. It wasn't until after we moved in that I realized something. The house we chose was the exact same floor plan as the home I'd lived in for most of my life. There was a familiarity to it that was comfortable, but there was also an undercurrent of discomfort of which I had not previously been conscious.

This is sometimes what happens in our marriages. We are drawn to certain patterns or ways of relating with our mates and our families because of the familiarity, but at the same time there may be subtle discontent with such patterns. We end up "moving into" the patterns simply because they feel comfortable in some ways and because we are not fully aware of what is causing the discontent or how to remedy it.

As we examine the essential aspects of proper leaving, keep in mind that you may be comfortable with what has been familiar in your family, but you may need to face the discomfort of change. Following God's guidelines for establishing a healthy marriage may require some adjustment or rethinking on both your and your mate's parts. Be prayerful and open as you read, and ask God for His perspective and wisdom as you apply His principles in your marriage.

PHYSICALLY LEAVING
(BODY)

It is true that physically leaving your parents' home is essential to the formation of a good marriage. But what does it mean? In the physical realm, we move out from under our parents' covering of shelter, financial dependence, and authority. A shift is supposed to take place. We are no longer to look to our parents to provide for our physical or financial needs. We are to separate and establish a home where our primary responsibility is first to God and then to our spouse and eventually to our children.

Several years ago, Don and I attended a marriage retreat presented by Ron and Betty Wiseman called "Enjoying Marriage."

Ron showed an illustration that has been extremely helpful as I have counseled couples in this area of proper leaving and cleaving.[2]

Diagram 1: Married Person

Diagram 1 represents any married person. The centermost circle represents your highest relational priorities as made clear in Scripture. Your number-one priority is God, followed by your spouse, then your children and their mates, should they marry, and eventually your grandchildren. These are the relationships that should be paramount in your life. Your actions, not just your words, demonstrate the true priority these relationships have in your life. How much time, energy, and commitment do you invest in each relationship?

In the second circle are the relationships that are of secondary importance. They include your extended family, your parents, grandparents, brothers and sisters, and all other relatives. Also included in this circle might be close, intimate friends with whom you have a deep, long-standing relationship that remains significant in your lives. These relationships are important, but they should never overshadow or take precedence over the relationships in your inner circle. In the outer circle belongs everyone else with whom you have a relationship. This may include casual friends and acquaintances, coworkers, or neighbors.

It is possible for someone in our outer circle to move to the middle circle, but it is not appropriate for anyone to penetrate that inner circle, and it is vital that we protect it.

Now here's an essential concept. When our sons and daughters marry, they continue to be in our inner circle, and we add to our inner circle their mates and eventually their children. However, the minute they marry, *we, their parents, shift to their middle circle,* and we take second place to their spouse. We are among their relatives and close intimate relationships. Diagram 2 shows where Don and I will fit into the set of circles our daughters will draw. Our daughters, their husbands, and their children (our grandchildren) will always be in our inner circle. But when our daughters marry, we will move to their middle circle and *their* inner circle only consists of God, their mate, their children, and eventually their grandchildren.

Diagram 2: Your Married Son or Daughter

What does this mean practically? Ron Wiseman told a story that perfectly illustrates the lines of distinction that should be in place. He shared how both of his adult children and their mates are in his inner circle, and when they come home, they open the front door and say, "Hi, Mom and Dad — we're here!" His son may even go to the refrigerator and look inside for something to eat. "But," he says, "when we go over to our son's house, we knock on the door or ring the doorbell and wait to be invited in." Even while in their home, "I would never go to the refrigerator without asking permission."[3]

This kind of respect acknowledges and supports a marriage. I have counseled several couples whose parents have not respected boundary lines. That behavior tends to weaken the marital bond and causes a division of loyalties. Throughout our lives, we are to continue to honor our parents and the position God gave them in our lives, but once we are married, our primary allegiance and responsibility is to our mate. Honoring our parents means we may seek their counsel and respect their opinions because they have lived longer and know us well. Honoring our parents means we may need to provide care for them as they age. But we are not required to follow their advice, and we are especially not to oppose our mate in deference to our parents.

CULTURAL DIFFERENCES

For some of you, this may be a troubling notion. Many cultures differ in practice when it comes to the relationship with parents and the extended family. For instance, in the Asian culture, parents and extended family are revered and viewed as an integral part of the family system. They would be seen in that inner circle illustrated earlier. It is not uncommon for married adult children to live in their parents' home and to include their parents in decision making. In Latin cultures, the extended family is highly involved in the raising of children, and family gatherings are open events in which all relatives are always welcome. However, Latin families are more fluid, and their requirement to adhere to parental advice after marriage is not as expected as in the Asian culture.

Understanding your mate's ethnic/cultural history is of vital importance. Many Anglo-Americans are unaware and unaccustomed to family traditions and mores that are understood in other cultures. Because of the diversity of our culture, these differences may remain in the background before marriage, but they often emerge in the years that follow.

Michael and Keiko met each other while attending college. Even though Keiko was raised in the United States, her parents were immigrants. Michael was initially enamored of Keiko's rich Japanese heritage. He was raised in Brooklyn by hardworking parents who had little time for parenting their five boys. Michael was on his own from the time he was about twelve. Although Michael and Keiko were very much in love, problems began to emerge in their marriage over decision making. Whether it was choosing a house to buy or where they should send their children to school, Keiko felt tremendous guilt if she did not consult her parents. During their courtship, Michael saw this pattern as respectful on Keiko's part, and he assumed she would transfer to him that same consideration once they were married. He was wrong. He soon discovered that their cultural differences were creating strife that he had not bargained for.

Being aware of these differences and integrating the biblical mandate to "leave behind" father and mother can be challenging—

but not impossible. When God set forth these principles to His people, Israel, they lived in clans and were expected to respect and follow the elders who led their families and community. At the same time, they were encouraged and required to establish their own family unit, which was to be honored among the community. In biblical times when a man married, he was not to be "sent to war or have any other duty laid on him," but for an entire year he was to "stay at home and bring happiness" to the wife he married (Deuteronomy 24:5). From these and other passages, we can be assured that God esteems the marriage relationship, and His Word transcends cultures. You may need the help of someone who both is knowledgeable about cultural issues and has a healthy, practical understanding of God's Word and intent for marriage. The goal in establishing boundaries is not exclusion but protection for the sacred bond you have entered into before God.

EMOTIONALLY LEAVING
(SOUL)

Couples commonly overlook this area. They may have left physically, but unhealthy emotional ties remain intact. There are two types of emotional entanglements that hinder proper leaving. The first is more obvious than the second. We refer to it as overt emotional attachment.

OVERT EMOTIONAL ATTACHMENT

Overt emotional attachment is at work when a married adult son or daughter continues to be tied emotionally to either parent in a way that observers can readily see. There is an over-involvement, a lack of appropriate separation, or a dependency (either financial or emotional) that keeps the adult child going back to the parent to meet needs.

This type of emotional attachment may involve the adult child playing the "rescuee" while the parents play the "rescuer." The adult child continually creates situations where Mom or Dad (or both) steps in to solve a problem or circumvent a consequence for their grown child. As a result, the adult child doesn't mature and learn how to be responsible for himself or his family. Usually this is a long-standing pattern that is not easily undone. One of the saddest aspects of this scenario is that the adult child often holds tremendous contempt for his parents. I have sat with many parents who didn't understand what had gone wrong. They had rescued their adult child time after time, thinking that someday responsible behavior was going to click in. They weren't prepared for the barrage of contempt that often followed their adult child's plea to be rescued "one more time."

Another common problem has to do with parents who have difficulty letting go. Jeff had always been close to his parents. He was a sensitive boy, and his mother was particularly in tune with her son's moodiness. When Jeff decided to marry in his early thirties, he talked extensively with his parents about everything. Jeff's fiancée, Erin, became increasingly concerned over his attachment to his mother and voiced her discomfort. Jeff thought Erin was overreacting.

Jeff's mother verbally supported his intention to marry but asked Jeff throughout his engagement if he was sure that Erin was the "right one" for him. After their marriage, Jeff would call his mother whenever he and Erin got into an argument to get his mom's perspective on things. Instead of encouraging Jeff to talk things out with Erin or suggesting Jeff see a counselor or pastor, his mother would reinforce Jeff's dependency because of *her need to be needed.* She would reassure him by saying that she understood him better than anyone else and that the conflicts had more to do with Erin than with him.

On the surface, these "need to be needed" parents may support leaving, but underneath they encourage emotional dependence. There is a subtle message that says, "Please don't leave me." Sometimes there is a subconscious fear that without the "child" to focus on, the parent may lose his or her identity altogether or fall apart.

Most of us have heard about a man who is "still tied to his mother's apron strings" or a daughter who is "still holding on to her father's coattails." These bonds are developed over time and do not disappear automatically. They can easily create tension in a marriage and be an obstacle to bonding with a mate.

If a married adult child consistently seeks his or her primary source of emotional support from a parent rather than his or her mate, help may be needed. Emotional leaving requires a shift in allegiance and dependence.

As an adult child, you protect your marriage by not allowing yourself to be manipulated by guilt or pressured into situations where you must choose between your parent and your mate. One way to know you have successfully mastered leaving emotionally is when your relationship with your parents has transitioned from a parent/child relationship to an adult/adult relationship. This means the interactions are no longer based on parental authority but on mutual respect that exists between two adults. It doesn't mean that you stop loving or respecting your parents. As adult children, you honor your parents but realize your marital bond is the one that must have top priority.

I have seen many families where this principle has been respected on both sides. The result is a very close family that remains dedicated and devoted to one another while maintaining a healthy respect for separateness.

Tom and Christy had this kind of family. Christy's parents lived about five miles away and her siblings lived within close proximity. Tom and Christy's three children had a warm relationship with their grandparents, aunts, uncles, and cousins. Holidays were great family times, but Christy's parents, Carol and Rick, never insisted that all their children be at every event. They often made adjustments out of consideration for their children and their growing families. They were available to lend support when Tom was injured on the job and required hospitalization. During that time, they cared for the grandchildren, supplied needed meals, and saw to it that Christy could spend as much time at the hospital as she needed. Even aside from special circumstances, Carol and Rick were quick to ask how they could be of support, but they were very respectful about not being intrusive. They also knew how to maintain their own marriage by not living *for* their children and grandchildren, but continuing to grow and enhance their relationship. Christy and Tom felt they had the freedom to call on Carol and Rick at any time, but they knew Mom and Dad honored their marriage enough not to interfere in conflicts or decisions without being asked. When a family operates within these guidelines, it fosters growth, love, and security.

COVERT EMOTIONAL ATTACHMENT

The second emotional entanglement that hinders a proper "leaving" is what I call *covert emotional attachment*. This attachment is subtle and may actually *appear* to be healthy separation because it looks like the opposite of overt emotional attachment. This emotional attachment exists internally and is usually the result of unresolved family-of-origin issues that occupy thought or emotional energy. It may not show itself until it is activated or threatened.

An example may help. We shared in an earlier chapter that during our courtship, Don's pastor, Mike, observed that Don was still emotionally attached to his family. Pastor Mike did not know much about my background, and on the surface it looked as though I had made a healthy break from my family. In reality, I was more "covertly" attached. I had established my own life separate from my parents but lived emotionally connected to them by the unresolved abuse issues from my past. This attachment did not manifest itself immediately, but it was in place, ready to influence our marriage.

How might you know if you are covertly emotionally attached? One way is to measure how much attention or mental energy you invest in thinking about your family of origin. Do you mull over events, think through conversations, or imagine how a situation might have been different if you had acted differently? This regular replaying of events can be a signal that the issues have not been resolved.

Another sign that is a bit more difficult to detect is avoidance. You don't *ever* want to think about the things that happened in your family. "It's over and done with, and I've handled it."

Both Don and I spent a great deal of energy trying not to deal with our past. We were out from under our parents' roofs and were independent, self-sufficient adults — or so we thought. Neither of us initially realized how much of our energy was tied up with our parents and the issues of growing up.

This is true for many people. They think because they have moved three thousand miles across the country to "get away" from the family, they have successfully left. Unfortunately, many still live in reaction against their pasts or continue the emotional entanglement with their pasts, even if estranged from their families. A person may be covertly attached even when he has little or no contact with his family.

"We do things, by and large, as we saw them done or as a *reaction to* the ways we saw them done, and this tendency to behave in *reverse* ways is especially evident in certain emotionally charged situations," writes Maggie Scarf. She adds that even though we are acting completely differently than our parents did, we have "turned the behavior inside out." "One does the opposite, and in the next generation it boomerangs."[4] There is no resolution because each generation avoids working to resolve the real issue. Each lives out a reactive response that perpetuates the problem and passes it on.

Have you ever known someone who was brought up in a rigid family or legalistic church environment? You can often spot them in adulthood. They are the ones who are extremely vocal and reactive against anything "religious." They take pride in their separation from such a "confining, stifling system" and live in total contrast to their upbringing. Although these people might say they have disavowed everything from their family's religiosity and have *chosen* to live their life "their way," they are deceived. The truth is, these men and women are not *thoughtfully* choosing in freedom. They are living their lives *in reaction* to the system they are still subconsciously rebelling against. As a result, they are truly not free agents but are still tied to their past in that they are reacting to it. They attest to being out from under the oppressive cloak and may appear to have shed all traces of their family's values, but they have not really left. They make daily choices that are dictated by what they think they have left behind. The choices are in direct opposition to the former system, but they are made from the emotional attachment that is covertly operating beneath the surface.

Leaving one's family emotionally means separating from any *emotional dependence* or *reactive independence*. This may not mean that the minute you marry, you make an immediate transfer. Leaving takes a process of time. However, there must be evident progressive steps and a mindset that allows and promotes such leaving.

We've discussed leaving physically and emotionally; now let's look into spiritual leaving.

SPIRITUALLY LEAVING
(SPIRIT)

Leaving your father and mother spiritually does not mean that you forsake your spiritual heritage or the foundations of your faith established in your home growing up. It does mean that you make your faith your own. As adults, we are responsible before God to establish our own adult relationship with God. As I heard a pastor once say, "God doesn't have grandchildren." We cannot depend on our parents' or grandparents' faith, no matter how strong our family's legacy of faith might be.

Spiritual leaving sometimes involves exploring your spiritual heritage as an individual and as a couple. Don and I had diverse spiritual backgrounds. As single adults, we both broke away from our denominational roots as we established our own adult relationships with God. When we were dating we attended two different churches with very different worship styles. Both churches strongly emphasized God's Word. However, Don chose a traditional worship style and family-oriented congregation that fit more easily with his background. I chose a more contemporary style with an emphasis on evangelism and outreach. When we married we prayed about where God wanted us, and we discussed our preferences. We compromised and made some adjustments as we considered each other's needs and values. Both of our families were disconcerted that we had left the churches in which we grew up, but we knew this was an important step for our spiritual growth and the establishment of our own family unit.

Not every couple needs to leave the church in which they grew up. But as a couple becomes one, they will need to discover how best to encourage each other's spiritual growth, even if it means a break from the traditions established in their homes as they grew up. As Don and I had children, we had to reassess our family's needs and values again, taking into consideration the needs of our children and their growth as well as our own.

As a Christian, you are accountable to God for your spiritual growth. One particular form of that accountability involves seeking God for wisdom as to where He wants to place you in the body of Christ. In 1 Corinthians 12:18, Paul wrote, "But now God has placed the members, each one of them, in the body, *just as He desired*" (NASB, emphasis added). God's Word is clear that our purpose in the body is to glorify God and edify each other. In Ephesians 4:12-13, Paul added that God gave gifts to members of the body "to prepare God's people for service, so that the body of Christ may be built up until we all reach unity in the faith and in the knowledge of the Son of God and become mature, attaining to the whole measure of the fullness of Christ."

In other words, our involvement in the body of believers matters to God. We should not belong simply out of obligation or tradition, nor should we approach our church attendance and involvement in a casual, flippant manner. Recently, a friend of mine was asked about some problems in her church. Had she considered going elsewhere because of the conflict? She matter-of-factly said, "I'm married to this church." This kind of attitude promotes commitment.

Spiritual leaving requires first that we carefully examine what is behind our spiritual affiliation — has it simply been adopted from our history or have we taken personal ownership of our spiritual journey as an adult? Second, it means that we need to seek God about where He would have us connect and serve. It may mean we stay where our roots are, or it may mean we leave behind certain loyalties as God calls us elsewhere. This leaving may unnerve our families, but Jesus talked about the importance of following Him even when it meant there would be divisions among family members (see Matthew 10:35-37).

I once encountered a situation like this as I worked with a couple who had different religious upbringings. Phil and Cathy had made a commitment to Christ and wanted to bring up their young children in a solid Christian home. There was one problem. Phil no longer attended the church he had grown up in. He, Cathy, and their children attended another church that they believed adhered more closely to God's Word and seemed to be the right fit for their growing family. Phil's mother felt hurt every time her son talked about his church. She put him on a royal guilt trip each holiday as she made it a personal issue. She told him he was rejecting her and all the values she had tried to instill in his and his brother's lives.

While Phil was the "bad son," his brother, Bob, who continued attending the "family's" church, was the "good son." Phil's
mother looked beyond the fact that Bob was living an immoral
life, had a child outside of marriage, and was dishonest in business. She emphasized following tradition and made this an issue
of "family loyalty." Phil's mother was caught in what Jesus
referred to as "the tradition of men." She was more interested in
the outside appearance than what was really going on in the
hearts of her sons.

Phil realized his need to establish separateness from his
mother in this and other areas, as the connection was harming his
marital relationship. Spiritually leaving didn't mean he had to forsake all that he valued from his religious training. In fact, he and
his wife discussed the issue and compromised in order that he
could participate in certain religious events he found particularly
meaningful at his family's church. But he had to leave some of
the traditions and loyalties behind in order to pursue and protect
his own family's spiritual health and growth. He also had to learn
to leave behind his mother's guilt manipulation and make his
own decisions with strength and confidence.

FACING YOUR NEED TO LEAVE

We've looked at "leaving" as a three-dimensional process involving
the physical (body), emotional (soul), and spiritual (spirit) parts of
our makeup. As a result of reading this chapter, you may have discovered your own need to face certain areas in which proper leaving
has yet to take place. It's never too late to begin the process. You
may need to admit to God that your priorities have been out of
order. Tell Him you desire to follow Him first and put your mate
in his or her proper place. You may need to modify your loyalties

to your parents in order to follow God. You will discover as you read on how necessary leaving is to the process of cleaving.

ACTION STEP: SELF-REFLECTION

Below are some questions to ask yourself about your emotional separation from your parents. After you have answered the questions yourself, invite your spouse to answer them, with you and your family in mind. Then share with each other your observations.

1. Do you have an adult/adult relationship with your parents? (Do you still feel like a child? Do your parents treat you as one?)

2. Is your emotional energy invested more in your current family or in your family of origin? (Do you spend time mulling over your parents' issues or working hard to keep your relationship with them peaceful?)

3. Can you tolerate your parents' disapproval? (Can you go against their wishes without having undue emotional distress?)

4. Are you tied into family myths, secrets, or roles? (Do you comply with unspoken rules or roles just because that's the way it is supposed to be?)

5. Can you see your family in truth? (Do you deny reality for the sake of maintaining a certain accepted family image?)

CHAPTER 5

CLEAVING TO YOUR MATE

SPIRIT, SOUL, AND BODY

WHAT DOES IT MEAN TO CLEAVE TO YOUR MATE? IN HEBREW, the word for *cleave* means "to glue or cling." It implies bonding together like strong adhesive. I think God used this descriptive word to summon to our minds a vivid picture. If you've ever used Krazy Glue or another quick-bonding glue, you realize how essential it is to glue only what you intend to bond together! If you're like most of us, you have at one time or another inadvertently glued your finger or dripped some glue onto an unintended surface. It is almost impossible to pull apart that which has bonded together. If it is your fingers, that separation is also painful.

God designed marriage to be the same way. He called us to bond or cleave together so tightly that we feel pain when we try to disengage. This does not mean we enmesh with each other and become each other's identity. It does mean that we bond to one another on each level — body, soul, and spirit. We typically hear that the cleaving aspect of the marriage refers to physical bonding through the sexual relationship. This is only partly true. If cleaving does not take place on the other two levels, soul (emotional) and spirit, the relationship will show evidence of disrepair and a lack of intimacy.

A BONDING EXPERIENCE

I learned about bonding through an experience I had a few years ago.

While at a friend's home one day, I noticed that on the back of her bathroom door she had placed some decorative plastic hooks for towels. I went to the hardware store, purchased similar hooks, and was excited about having the extra space to hang towels in my daughters' bathroom. The hooks had adhesive on the back and came with detailed instructions that the surface on which the hooks were placed needed to be clean, smooth, and flat. I was anxious to get my hooks up and had no intention of sanding the surface. I brushed the surface of the door with one swipe, peeled back the paper from the adhesive, and pressed each hook into place. While swiping the door, I felt some slight ripples that had been painted over but rationalized that those ripples "probably would not matter." I held the hooks in place pressing firmly as directed and delayed hanging any towels on them for the prescribed twenty-four hours.

After bathing my daughters the next day, I proudly hung the lightweight towels on the hooks. A couple of days later, it happened. I found both towels along with the hooks on the bathroom floor. Attached to the adhesive were specks of dirt, hair, and tiny paint particles. The hooks could not bear the weight of the towels because the adhesive had not bonded properly.

Unwilling to accept defeat, I purchased more hooks and glued them on the door. A week went by this time before the fated day came. I was frustrated but realized that out of my enthusiasm (and laziness) I had failed to understand the importance of the clean, smooth surface in the bonding process.

As I reflected on this experience, I saw the value of the lesson as it relates to marriage. For us to bond properly with our mates, we must remove the debris. This is why looking at and dealing with your history is so important. With the hooks in my bathroom, all appeared to be working until the towels were placed on them. Then the weight exposed the lack of proper bonding. So it may be in your marriage. You may appear to be bonded together, but what happens when the stresses of life and the weight of trials and disappointments hit you?

For many, stress reveals the debris or baggage in areas that are contributing to a lack of bonding. You can remove some of this debris before marriage, but eventually the marriage itself reveals other areas where debris has accumulated. Learning to recognize and work through those areas provides the opportunity for cleaving to continue. That is what this book is about.

Below is a diagram that represents why it is important to deal with your history and the resulting debris.

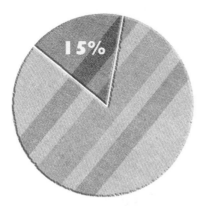 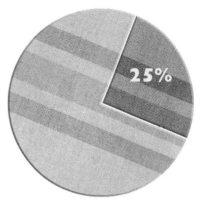

Circle A (male)   Circle B (female)

Circle A represents the male, and Circle B represents the female. The shaded areas represent the debris that each person has carried into the marriage from his or her background. As you learned in previous chapters, this debris may result from your unresolved childhood hurts, acts of commission or omission, or baggage from a previous marriage or relationship. As you can see, a sliver of this male's life falls into this category. Let's say this represents 15 percent of his emotional life. In Circle B, the female has a larger slice of life that has not been resolved or reconciled, which we'll say represents 25 percent of her emotional life. Now, let's superimpose those circles.

What you now see in diagram 2 is that 40 percent of this couple's life cannot bond together properly because there is too much debris. Like the hooks on my bathroom door, the marriage may not be able to withstand the weight of certain trials or life events because of this condition. The good news is that it is never too late for bonding to occur if we're willing to deal with the debris and ask God to help us reconcile our histories. In this way, we can cleave to our mate in the fullest measure.

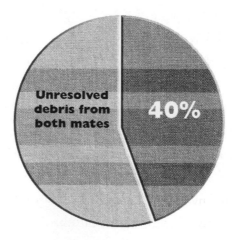

CLEAVING TO YOUR MATE 87

We will look at cleaving as a three-level process because like leaving, it is progressive. We'll talk about spiritual bonding as the *covenant* made between a man and a woman, emotional bonding as the *commitment* to one another, and physical bonding as the *communion* with one another.

SPIRITUAL BONDING
(COVENANT-SPIRIT)

When we marry, we enter into a covenant with our mate before God. Webster's defines *covenant* as a "binding agreement; a written agreement or promise usually under seal between two or more parties." The idea behind a covenant is that there are no loopholes. For cleaving to take place, there must be a sense of permanence. God has established a covenant with His people, Israel, which cannot be broken. Through the security of a covenant relationship, intimacy flourishes.

RESPECT INDIVIDUAL DIFFERENCES

What does spiritual bonding require? First of all, there must be a respect for each other's individual relationship with God. Marriage does not demand that our individual walks with God be identical. Your individual relationship with the person of Jesus Christ will reflect individual differences. Think of your relationship with others, especially with your children, if you have them. Your relationship with each child is unique. It reflects the uniqueness of your character and personality as well as the character and personality of the person with whom you are relating. So it is with God.

During my husband's and my premarital counseling, I became concerned about my having been a Christian much longer than Don; I felt that our religious backgrounds and training were too dissimilar. We varied in the way we prayed, worshiped, and had our devotional time. I went with these concerns to my pastor, who gave me some sound advice.

He said, "Don't focus on the differences. It is clear that both of you believe in the Lord Jesus and that you seek to have Him as the center of your home and relationship. Don't make these other things an issue, Jan, but choose to love, honor, and respect Don's relationship with the Lord as separate from yours."

I see many couples struggle in this area. The wife complains that her husband is not the "spiritual leader" in the relationship. The husband is angry because his wife "is not submitting to him as unto the Lord." Most of us become experts at what the other is failing to do, rather than focusing on what we are individually called to do!

Respecting our mate's walk with God means that we are not constantly evaluating his or her spirituality, because evaluation tends to undermine the relationship. Rather, we are prayerfully trusting God to work in his or her heart. Certainly, there are vital, uncompromising doctrinal issues that must be agreed upon if marital harmony is to be achieved. However, there are other aspects, characteristics, and doctrinal issues within the Christian faith in which we may differ, but not allow to become focal points of dissension.

The mutual respect Don and I have for our individual relationships with our Lord has proven over the years to bond us together. We have such freedom and support in this area because we trust each other and trust God within both of us to lead, correct, and instruct us as we seek Him individually and as a couple.

CULTIVATE SPIRITUAL GROWTH

In addition to the respect of each other's individual relationship with God, spiritual bonding requires that we spend time cultivating spiritual growth as a couple through prayer, sharing of God's Word, discussion, and accountability.

Prayer especially has enriched our life as a couple. We have not been model pray-ers by any means, but we have deepened in that area, and it has brought an intimacy and closeness that enhances other areas of our life. Sometimes I wish I could communicate to men how significant this area is for most women. It is not the eloquence or the subject of the prayer that matters, but it is hearing your mate's deepest desires, confession of wrong, tender concerns, and heartfelt cries that bring you together. As you open your hearts together before God, it's as if He weaves you together in Him. Ecclesiastes 4:12 says, "A cord of three strands is not quickly broken."

There is something so warming to my heart when Don shares with me a verse that has been particularly meaningful to him in his quiet time. And there are days when I e-mail him at work with a quote and verse from my own morning devotions that lift his heart.

Accountability with one another is just as valuable as praying together. The Bible tells us that "as iron sharpens iron, so one man sharpens another" (Proverbs 27:17).

I remember that early in our marriage, it seemed like a week could not go by without our having some type of interpersonal conflict. Since I am the "conflict-resolver" in our relationship, I am usually the one who brings the issue to the table. I remember Don saying at one point, "Do we have to deal with this stuff every week? Can't we have a week where things go smoothly now and then?" To my husband's chagrin, I replied emphatically, "Don, if you think I married for mediocrity, you're wrong. My job is to encourage and challenge you to be the best man of God that you can be — and I want you to do the same for me." My dear peace-loving husband hung his head for a moment and then quipped, "Tell me again — what's so wrong with mediocre?"

There have been many times in the last twenty-three years that we have had to "speak the truth in love" (Ephesians 4:15) to one another for the purpose of growth. I wish I could tell you that each of us always handled the truth graciously as the recipient. We haven't! But we have learned that we both have a strong commitment to be all that God has called us to be. We realize that God has chosen our marriage and each other to play a significant role in shaping us. In his book entitled *Sacred Marriage*, author Gary Thomas writes, "What if God designed marriage to make us holy more than to make us happy?"[1] Quite a provocative thought, isn't it?

"Spiritual growth is the main theme; marriage is simply the context."[2] As Don and I have yielded to God and each other, we have benefited and grown in grace and love. Now let's look at emotional bonding, because it is the bridge to physical intimacy, especially for women.

EMOTIONAL BONDING (COMMITMENT-SOUL)

What comes to your mind when you hear someone say, "That man is really committed to his family"? Or "She's a committed mother"? Or "That athlete is committed to the game"? Does commitment imply only that you put something or someone in a position of priority? Or is there something more?

After asking myself these questions and observing other marriages, I concluded that emotional bonding requires commitment. Yet commitment involves not only priority, but also action. Commitment involves action that is stimulated by a strong belief. In fact, *commitment is the covenant in action.*

When commitment is limited to putting something or someone in a position of priority without a purposeful plan of action, it is subject to stagnation. I know a couple whose marriage lasted forty-six years. They were committed to their relationship on the basis of years together. Yet if you looked behind closed doors, you'd find they had not shared a bed or bedroom for over ten years. They ate meals separately, had very little meaningful conversation, went few places together other than family functions, had no friends their own age, took separate vacations, and had not expressed or demonstrated affection for as long as either could remember. Staying together under such circumstances is commendable, but it is far less than what God intended for marriage.

As we gathered our thoughts for this book, Don and I talked about commitment. "It's more than just putting in time—like clocking in and out," he said. "You 'do time' in prison because you have no other options. Marriage should never be a place where you just put in time." God designed marriage to be fulfilling and rewarding. If we're committed, actively pursuing a purposeful plan toward oneness, we will experience the realization of His promises.

Commitment: On and Off the Court

Since Don coached basketball for twenty-eight years, I have been around a lot of players. I have learned the lingo, suffered through the losses, rejoiced at the victories, and become accustomed to the game and what it takes to play. I've even enjoyed it! Don and I have had lots of discussion over the years about different aspects of the game, including players, coaches, and various philosophies of what it takes to be successful. I've learned a lot about life from listening to Don share about coaching and being an athlete.

I asked Don once, "What does it mean when you say 'that player is committed to the game'?"

He said with assurance, "It's a player who goes beyond what is expected of him because he desires to be the best he can be. It's a guy who works on his game even when the coach is not around."

"What does all that involve?" I asked.

"He trains. He works on his weaknesses, hones his strengths, does all that he can to improve and keep improving. He prepares himself for competition. He prepares for the game mentally and emotionally, as well as physically."

"What do you mean mentally and emotionally?" I questioned.

"Jan, an athlete must be both mentally tough and emotionally ready to compete. An athlete can go through all the right things physically but still not have the emotional edge that is necessary to be all he can be. He has to play on an emotional edge. The athlete has to be emotionally into the game."

"Honey, how do you teach them that?"

"That's a good question. I've coached lots of young men. Some have all the technique and even great athletic ability, but if they don't have heart, their effort will be average. I've also had players with less talent who had heart. They play with an emotional edge to their game and they make up for their lack of skill. They may never be star players, but I'd rather have a player with heart and limited ability than a great player with no heart."

He went on to add, "It's a difficult thing to teach players to play with an emotional edge. We try to help them learn in practice how to play that way so they can duplicate it in a game situation. Sometimes I stop practice and compare when they were playing flat to when they were playing with emotion. I blow the whistle and say, 'Stop. Focus right now on how you're feeling—this is what I'm talking about. You're playing with emotion. If you can learn to duplicate this in a game, you will be a better player, and it will make us a better team.'"

Don looked thoughtfully at me and then added, "All those things he does for himself. The final two characteristics of a fine, committed athlete are that he is committed to the team and he is teachable. He is willing to make plays to help the team, even if it means personal sacrifice. A team player is hard to find. The ones with a teachable attitude we call 'coachable.' They are a cut above the rest. They don't have an 'I know it all' attitude, and they allow the coach to instruct them. These are the guys you can count on in the gut of the game—they'll come through for you with all they've got."

Working Together for the Good of the Team

Couples committed to marriage are like athletes committed to the team. Their commitment is not just a physical relationship in which either or both partners go through the motions. It is an emotional commitment that requires each spouse working to become the best he or she can be. They acquaint themselves with their own weaknesses, enhance their strengths, develop a mindset for doing their part in strengthening the marriage, and are amenable to learning from their mate, as well as from God, about the ways in which they can improve. They work for the good of the team.

Paul used the analogy of an athlete in 1 Corinthians 9:24-27 when he wrote about life as a Christian and what it requires:

> Do you not know that in a race all the runners run, but only one gets the prize? Run in such a way as to get the prize. Everyone who competes in the games goes into strict training. They do it to get a crown that will not last; but we do it to get a crown that will last forever. Therefore I do not run like a man running aimlessly; I do not fight like a man beating the air. No, I beat my body and make it my slave so that after I have preached to others, I myself will not be disqualified for the prize.

Paul was telling us to run with purpose and not just go through the motions. So many couples end up "running aimlessly" through married life. There is little passion in their relationship, and their life together lacks vitality. What would your marriage look like if you were to "run in such a way as to get the prize"? What elements are necessary to create the kind of emotional bonding that keeps a marriage strong?

FOCUSED TIME

Emotional bonding requires two crucial elements: focused time and vulnerability. We have to spend focused time with each other to emotionally bond. Very few of us feel connected when one sits in front of the television and the other behind a newspaper, even when dialogue ensues.

What does focused time involve? It means you purposefully set aside time to express interest in your mate's well-being. This does not mean the casual "How was your day?" as you're moving from one room to another. It means you are *really* interested, and you demonstrate that interest by the kinds of questions you ask and the attention you give.

I tried an experiment with Don once. We were both going through a stressful time. One night I asked him to tell me the two things that were weighing *most* heavily on my heart at the time. He mentioned two things that were of concern to me, but they weren't the central issues of my heart. I turned to Don and told him what I thought were the two things weighing most heavily on him and asked if I was right. I was.

Now I know some of you men reading this are saying, "Of course. You women are just better at that kind of stuff than we men." The truth is, women may have more natural ability in this area, but this interest is a skill that can be developed and learned, much like the athlete who lacks natural athleticism. It takes expending effort, being teachable, and tuning in.

Most men would make the effort if they could see it made a difference. I have good news — it does. The marriages that have a strong spiritual and emotional connection flourish in the physical/sexual area as well. Because most women need emotional connection before engaging in the sexual arena, husbands who learn to foster spiritual and emotional connectedness find their wives more open and interested in lovemaking.

VULNERABILITY

Along with focused time when sincere interest and caring are expressed, vulnerability is another vital component in the development of emotional bonding. Vulnerability simply means sharing your real self.

I remember several years ago, when our children were young,

we were traveling back to our home from San Diego late one evening. Don was driving, and the girls had fallen asleep in the backseat of the car. I'm not sure what started the conversation, but Don began sharing with me spontaneously about the coaches who had influenced his life. He talked about his Little League coach, his Pony League coach, a basketball coach he had in college, and another man whom he had coached alongside. For over an hour he shared about those men, their impact on his life, what he learned from each one, and how athletics had taught him about life. I asked questions at appropriate times, but for the most part I just listened. That car ride is stellar in my mind. When we arrived home that evening, I felt so close to my husband. I felt as though he had pulled back a curtain in his heart and invited me into his inner chamber. I felt so privileged to be connected to him, and I wanted to be more intimate. Even though the content of the conversation had no romantic tone, it created intimacy because of the nature of Don's vulnerability. If men only knew how women love and respond to this!

It doesn't mean men can fake either of these elements — women are very in tune to counterfeit interest shown or pseudo-vulnerability that is a maneuvering effort. And don't think for a minute that women are the only ones who need this kind of bonding. Men need it, too. For men, emotional bonding involves encouragement, expressed admiration and respect, and demonstration that they are loved and needed.

Peter was a successful businessman. He and Jenny had been married about ten years. Both had been divorced and came into marriage with a lot of baggage. Peter's first wife, Ann, was extremely controlling and ambitious. Jenny's previous husband had been financially irresponsible and unfaithful. About seven years into Peter and Jenny's marriage, Peter's business collapsed and prospects looked grim. Peter's self-esteem hit an all-time low, and Jenny feared what the future might hold. Instead of letting her past dictate her response, she set out to encourage Peter. She told him how much she respected his business sense and how his integrity did not falter even under the stress of losing his business. She encouraged him to take some time off to consider what God would have him do next and not to feel pressured to take any job that came along. She said if need be, they could sell their home (which she loved) and downsize in order to relieve him of some of the financial burden. Peter felt like a ton of weight had been lifted from his shoulders. Jenny's response helped him feel that she was with him in the crisis and that he was emotionally supported.

When we talk about emotional bonding, we are not saying that men need to be like women in terms of the way they communicate. But both partners do need to be aware of the emotional aspect of their makeup. Our God is full of emotion. If you doubt this, just study the life of Jesus. God created emotions and wants us to learn how to properly integrate them for our own health and well-being.

Emotional bonding fosters our commitment because we are spending focused time with our mate, showing genuine interest and concern, and sharing our real self with him or her. This starts in the dating process and must continue throughout the marriage if it is to stay strong and flourish.

PHYSICAL BONDING
(COMMUNION-BODY)

Have you ever wondered why God created sex? I sure have. But I don't have a definitive answer. What I do know is that God said it is good, it is for a man and woman within the confines of marriage, it is for the purpose of reproducing, it is to be engaged in regularly within the marriage, it is to be enjoyed, it creates oneness and depicts oneness, it symbolizes the relationship between Christ and His church, and it is a mystery.

I have linked physical bonding with communion because *communion means intimate fellowship or rapport.* I have purposely talked about physical bonding last because I believe the richness of our physical relationship in marriage is the expression of the bonding that has been enhanced on the spiritual and emotional levels. We will talk more about the sexual relationship and the history partners bring to it in chapters 8 and 9.

How does physical bonding relate to cleaving? Physical bonding does not just pertain to the sexual aspect of the relationship. In fact, most couples whose sexual relationship is flourishing will tell you that they have regular times of affection and physical contact that do not aim at sexual release. There are times when they hold hands; hug; give back rubs; sit beside one another; and show tenderness, affection, and care through touch. It is most interesting that some of the things that we regularly practice in dating and courtship disappear after marriage. It's no wonder couples struggle with intimacy and sexual satisfaction.

Think about it: In your dating, you spend hours talking, showing interest in the other by asking questions, intently listening, paying close attention to what pleases the other, finding unique ways to express your tenderness toward the other, and showing appropriate nonsexual affection. For some, the minute they get married this goes out the window, and the couple can't figure out where the excitement and anticipation has gone.

God made the physical, emotional, and spiritual aspects within us to work together in harmony. The reality is that at times, in all of our marriages, we are out of sync with one another in at least one or more of these areas. Sometimes an illness, pregnancy, or stress prevents us from bonding physically as much as at other times. But when a couple has learned to nurture each other in alternate ways, these periods of abstinence are weathered more easily.

A common complaint expressed in marital counseling has to do with the frequency of sex. Let's look at how two different couples handled this dilemma.

Joe and Denise had been married five years. Joe became discouraged because it seemed like each year Denise's interest in lovemaking seemed to decrease. They talked openly about her lack of desire and began exploring their histories, facing and tracing the sources of influence on their current sexual desires or lack thereof. They communicated about the difference in their desires and the roots of those differences, and this communication opened for them a whole new understanding of each other. When Denise said no to sex, Joe could handle it because he wasn't taking it as a personal rejection. He understood how important it was for Denise to feel loved and cared for outside of the sexual arena because of her history of sexual abuse, and he could share with her some of his own frustration. He reassured Denise through listening to her, praying together, spending quality time with her, and showing affection through nongenital touch.

Denise felt Joe's tender concern for her and opened her heart to him in new ways. She asked Joe how she might express love to him in other ways to meet some of his needs as well. She found herself wanting to respond to Joe's physical and emotional needs the more they shared and communicated with each other.

Together, Joe and Denise were committed to finding a way to make sex work for both of them. As they navigated through these troubled waters, they discovered that their relationship had grown in ways they had not anticipated. They were bonded at a deeper level: spiritually, emotionally, and physically.

How different this was for Gary and Tricia. They were married six years when Gary announced that if Tricia didn't start responding to his sexual needs, he might have to "go elsewhere" and it would be her fault. Tricia was disgusted with Gary's demands and often busied herself late at night to avoid his advances. When they did have sex, Tricia felt disconnected and Gary seemed interested only in having his needs met. Tricia resented him and found her mother's words echoing in her mind — *men are only interested in one thing.* Deep down, Gary felt undesirable, but instead of sharing his feelings of rejection with Tricia, he would quote Scripture, telling her she had a responsibility to meet his needs. Gary and Tricia were going nowhere fast. The problem in Gary and Tricia's relationship was not primarily a sexual one — that was only the symptom. Both Gary and Tricia had histories that were contributing to a host of problems in their relationship, and unless they were willing to begin addressing this problem by facing their histories, the couple's chances for sustaining a marriage were slim.

MEETING IN THE MIDDLE

You may have noted that when we talked about leaving, we started with the physical and ended with the spiritual, and that in this section on cleaving, we've done exactly the opposite. We started with the spiritual and ended with the physical. If we put this in diagram form it would look like this:

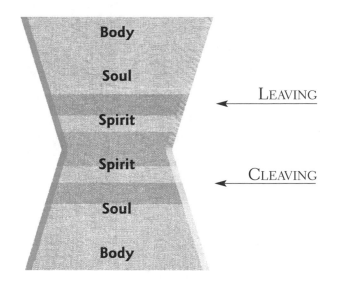

The top half of the hourglass represents leaving, and the bottom half represents cleaving. Notice that at the center, we are the closest. The true essence and eternal part of who we are is spiritual in nature. All of these components of leaving and cleaving on the levels of body, soul, and spirit work together to create the oneness that God designed for marriage.

BECOMING ONE

Becoming one flesh is both an immediate and a progressive step. The minute we take our vows before God, we are "one flesh"—but as we live together in a Christ-centered relationship we become more "one" than when we first said, "I do."

This progressive oneness does not occur automatically. "A good marriage is not something you find, it's something you work for."[3]

The oneness of marriage is pleasing to God. In Genesis 2:25 it says, "The man and his wife were both naked and they felt no shame." It is a mystery to me that God finds pleasure in that oneness, but He does. He wants you to experience the fullness of what He designed marriage to be.

Leaving and cleaving are essential elements of your present patterns that you need to face in order to experience the fullness of marriage. Other patterns include the issues you identified in your assessment (chapter 3). Now that you've faced all of this, you may be wondering what to do with it! The next step is to *trace* those present patterns to past events.

ACTION STEP: DIALOGUE WITH YOUR MATE

We've talked about two essential ways to enhance emotional bonding: focused time and vulnerability. At least three times this week, set aside fifteen minutes to focus on your mate's needs. Ask your mate some specific questions:

1. How can I best support you at this time? (Ask for specific ways, such as giving a back rub, following up on paying an overdue bill, having dinner ready on time, or arranging for a baby-sitter for the kids.)

2. About what can I pray for you specifically this week?

3. How can I express my love to you this week in a way that is particularly meaningful in light of what you are facing?

At the end of the week, ask your mate to share how these questions and your responses helped him or her feel encouraged during the week.

CHAPTER 6

HISTORY REPEATING ITSELF

TRACING

I T'S BEEN SAID, "THOSE WHO DO NOT KNOW HISTORY ARE forever condemned to repeat it." Sometimes, even when you know your history, it replays itself.

I remember that as a child I intensely disliked hearing a phrase my mother often used. If I was whining or crying longer than the situation called for, my mother would say, "Stop crying or I'll give you something to cry about." I remember thinking as I got older how much I resented that threat! I vowed when I became a parent I would never use such tactics.

Then the day came. My daughter Heather was crying over something insignificant in my eyes, and out of my mouth came — "Stop crying or I'll . . . " I turned an immediate about-face, convinced my mother had followed me there! I realized then that my history would automatically repeat itself unless I was purposeful in my desire to change. As Charles Sell wrote in his book *Unfinished Business*, "I knew that I had left home, but home had not left me."[1]

How does *your* history play itself out in your daily life? There are probably countless examples each day in which you replicate your history. It may be as simple as the way you do the breakfast dishes or whether or not you close your dresser drawers after retrieving your socks. Facing the fact that your history *is* very much incorporated into your life and relationships is the first step, and now you're ready for the next step of *tracing* your history.

Tracing involves understanding how present patterns are tied to past events. It means that you face a current pattern and trace it to its origin. For instance, when you took the assessment in chapter 3, you may have discovered that you answered "yes" to several questions relating to closeness and intimacy. Perhaps you identified with guarding your heart against hurt and keeping your needs and feelings to yourself. In tracing, then, you will ask yourself the question, *Where did this pattern of behavior or way of thinking come from?*

You might use the road map that you created as a reference point at which to begin. Were there any events or circumstances in your life that contributed to your pattern of protecting yourself from hurt? As you look over the road map, you might see one significant event or a series of events. Or you might not see an event at all but instead notice that one of the contributing factors was an omission. Maybe in your family, feelings were not shared. You kept your emotions to yourself because your parents had difficulty expressing their emotions and the family environment didn't foster emotional expression. As a result, it is difficult for you to communicate your feelings openly to your mate. Once you have faced the pattern and traced it to its roots, you are better equipped to understand how the pattern formed and then implement needed change.

For the purpose of this book, we are most concerned with any hurtful or unhealthy patterns that affect your relationships with your mate or family members. Think about your relationship with your mate. Where do most of your trouble spots appear? If you're like most of us, the three most common areas in which tension or conflicts arise are communication, money, and sex.

Before you start thinking about how offbase your mate is in any of these areas, take a side trip with me. Think for a moment about your family growing up. What was communication like between your parents? Does your communication style resemble that of either of your parents? How would you characterize that style — withdrawn, explosive, caring and sharing, noncommunicative, open? What is your mate's chief complaint in this area? Did you ever hear the same complaint voiced by either of your parents about the other in your family growing up?

What about money issues? Between your parents, who was the spender and who was the saver? Was the first of the month a tense time in your household? Who decided how the money was spent? How did your parents resolve conflicts over money? Are there any similar patterns in your relationship with your mate?

Most couples need to talk about sex. How did you learn about sex, and from whom? Were your parents a good resource of information for you in this area, or was sex a taboo subject? Have you had unpleasant sexual experiences either through abuse, dating, or a previous marriage? How do you feel about sex now? How do you and your mate differ in your attitudes toward sex?

Early in our marriage Don and I were discussing how we each learned about sex. Don said he learned about it from guys on the playground at school. His parents never talked openly with him about the subject. He, in turn, asked me about my experience. I shared how I was exposed to a graphic depiction of sex when I was ten and how disgusting this was to me. As a result of this and other factors, my attitude toward sex was tainted. I responded by avoiding closeness and making excuses for my lack of interest.

Through tracing, Don and I gained a better understanding of our histories, and we were able to talk openly about them with each other. Don was more compassionate as he realized the historical factors that contributed to my views regarding sex. Together we talked about ways to create a more positive experience with each other. We talked about what was healthy and what we wanted to do differently in teaching our own daughters about sexuality from a godly perspective. Attitudes and patterns like these do not change overnight, but with recognition and understanding, you are well on your way to alternatives.

When faced with these and other differences of history, many couples concentrate on whose family "did it the right way." Yet our purpose in tracing is not to blame our parents or our spouses. Nor is it to excuse ourselves. We use the information to understand our mates and ourselves. It is true that when we examine our histories, we often discover some unhealthy patterns or dysfunctional roots that need to be replaced with healthier ones. Our history has shaped us, but our God can reshape us as we yield ourselves to Him.

It is helpful to look at the patterns we bring into our marriage, trace them back to their roots, and evaluate them. Most of us have given little thought to these patterns before we marry. When we fail to look at them, we end up repeating patterns by default rather than purposeful implementation.

Tracing your history also involves determining what has value. Do you remember the couple in chapter 3 whose home was destroyed by fire? They needed to call in a restoration company to determine what parts of the structure could be saved—what, if anything, was valuable, what parts needed repair, and what needed replacement. As you trace your history, you might find it helpful to place patterns into the following categories:

- Valuable
- Repairable
- Replaceable

VALUABLE

In order to determine whether something is valuable, the restoration company must examine the damage carefully. For instance, if a bearing beam has suffered minor fire damage, they must evaluate whether that beam has incurred sufficient damage to compromise the integrity of the structure if they were to leave it. The bearing beam is designed to take the weight to the foundation, so if it is faulty, the structure is at great risk. Likewise, if you have suffered damage that directly affects your foundation as a person, you will be at greater risk.

Some foundational issues include your sense of worth (Were you esteemed as valuable, special, unique, and deserving of love in your home growing up?); your sense of belonging (Were you secure and protected, bonded and attached to the members of your family?); and your sense of competence (Were you nurtured and encouraged in achieving tasks/personal goals and affirmed in both your successes and failures?). These foundational issues influence your ability to navigate through the interpersonal differences and conflicts that arise in all relationships. If, when you took the assessment, you found you responded affirmatively to the questions about self-esteem and self-confidence, it will be helpful for you to take personal ownership by determining to obtain help for yourself on those issues.

In addition to these foundational issues, you'll want to evaluate the patterns of relating, belief systems, communication styles, and conflict resolution methods you observed or developed in your family of origin. Which ones are worth saving?

Think for a minute about your own background. What did you observe in your family that was valuable and worth imitating? Some of those things might include family traditions: caring for a needy family at holiday time, taking a family vacation each summer, opening your home to neighbors and friends for a Bible study, family devotions and prayer. Valuable attitudes might include a genuine respect for authority that was modeled and encouraged, an open atmosphere for discussing differences of opinion among family members, thoughtfulness and kindness to family members, or generosity to those in need. You might have observed relational patterns that you would want to emulate: your father consistently complimented your mother about her cooking; your parents regularly nurtured their relationship with time alone; courtesy and gratitude were expressed openly and often; a warmth and genuine "at home" feeling permeated your household. There may be many things that you want to continue as you develop your own family and nurture your own marriage.

One thing Don and I brought to our relationship was a good work ethic. We both knew what it meant to be hardworking adults putting ourselves through college. We were not afraid of an honest day's work. We also had similar ideas about what it meant to be a responsible adult — ideas that our parents had helped shape into our lives. One of the most admirable traits I saw in Don was his loyalty and integrity. He was and is a man of his word. This quality was and is extremely important to me. We both brought into our marriage a high level of commitment that served us well in our early years as we tackled tough issues. I brought with me a fierce tenacity to have our relationship become all that God intended it to be. And Don's gracious stability has calmed many a raging storm in our home over the years.

One of the best ways to assess whether something should be placed in the valuable category is to ask yourself if you would want your children to adopt the same pattern. If the answer is not a wholehearted "yes," it may be a pattern that needs to go into the repairable or replaceable categories. Valuable things are not necessarily things we do perfectly. They are useable, functional, and healthy as they serve to accomplish a desired goal. They are behaviors or traits that, when yielded to God, produce fruit in our lives now and in generations to come.

The concept of *when yielded to God* is crucial. Any character trait or behavior that is self-determined or perpetuated without the grace and sustaining power of God is susceptible to fleshly perversion, pious legalism, or religious dysfunction.

ACTION STEP: IDENTIFYING VALUABLES

Take a few minutes right now and ask the Holy Spirit to reveal to you what from your background is valuable. Write down on a separate sheet of paper the things you see that you want to continue in your relationship with your spouse and family. If you are single, this can be an important exercise for you as well.

Then do the same thing as you think about the background of your spouse or the person you are dating. What are valuable traits, patterns, and behaviors that you would want them to continue?

After completing your list, encourage your spouse, fiancée, or friend to do the same. Then compare your lists together, and use this exercise as a springboard for sharing your hearts. Pray over these lists and commit them to the Lord. Remember, "without [Him] you can do nothing" (John 15:5, NKJV).

As you review the two lists and combine them, think together about some additional creative ways you might work toward keeping the patterns or traits alive in your relationship and how you can encourage your children along the same pathway. If you find your lists of valuable items a bit thin, you may need to move to the next category, which is that of "repairable" items.

REPAIRABLE

To repair something is "to restore to a sound or healthy state."[2] To say that something needs repair suggests that the item is not in optimal condition. It may need a few minor adjustments, some strengthening, or a major overhaul. It has substance but needs improvement.

I find that many married couples have several areas in their relationship that are in this condition. However, for the most part, the individuals are unaware of their need to "repair."

One of the areas that couples commonly struggle with is communication. Most of us don't have a gadget that measures how we rate when it comes to good communication. We usually figure out we're not doing well in that area when we find ourselves in the heat of battle with our mate or in alone times when we feel the frustration of not being heard or understood.

Don and I knew that good communication was vital for sustaining a good marriage, but how did we measure up? We discovered early that both of us had some skill in communication. But we had faulty patterns that needed repair and other patterns that simply needed to be discarded and replaced. Let's look at some repairable items more closely.

Both Don and I came into marriage with good verbal skills. As an educator, Don had learned how to speak in front of a class and communicate information clearly. I had taken some speech courses and had worked in corrections, a field that required both written and verbal skills to provide information for the courts. We had a good foundation but needed to strengthen our skills at interpersonal communication. Talking with a spouse is less formal and more intimate than talking to students or judges. We had to learn how to talk to one another, and more important, how to listen. Since both of us were in professions in which we talked and the other person (his student, my probationer) were required to listen, we were more adept at "communicating to" each other rather than "with" each other. We had to learn to listen and paraphrase back to the speaker what we heard. Putting into words what we thought we heard helped us avoid misunderstandings. It slowed us down to hear rather than simply plan a retort. And it let each of us know that the other had heard.

We also needed to learn to be responsible for our own desires and for communicating them clearly to each other. I'll never forget the difficulty we used to have renting videos. I would go into the store looking for a video to rent for the evening. I would see a drama on the shelf that I really wanted to see. I'd pick it up and continue perusing what else was available. I would invariably run across a movie that I thought Don would probably enjoy more than the one I had chosen. He likes romantic comedies, classics, or historical dramas. I would pick up one of these and struggle for fifteen minutes over which movie to get. Invariably I chose the one I thought Don would like, rented it, and took it home. After putting the girls to bed, making popcorn, and settling in for the movie, I'd pop in the video. Within minutes, Don would fall asleep or lose interest in the comedy that I thought he'd love. I was miffed!

This scenario happened countless times for both of us. He would go to the video store and try to please me, only to be frustrated that I had no interest in what he had chosen. Finally, we made an agreement that saved us much frustration. We decided that whoever went to the video store could choose what they wished to see for the evening. If the mate at home had a specific request, they could offer that, but the one who was at the store made the final decision. We stopped trying to codependently please each other and took responsibility for our own choices and desires. What a world of difference this made. What is so amazing is how long it took us to figure out such a simple solution!

There are other areas in your marriage that may need to be repaired: anger management, financial responsibility, parenting, conflict resolution, or sex. Facing and tracing these issues will help you gain a better understanding of each other and then take steps toward change.

However, what do we do when we find ourselves in destructive patterns that have no redeeming value? We learn first to recognize them and then to replace them.

REPLACEABLE

If we're honest, most of us know we bring into adulthood some dysfunctional patterns or character flaws that need to be discarded or changed. It's essential to make the distinction between what is repairable (something needing restoration or improvement) and those areas that are no longer useful and need to be replaced (banished, forsaken, or nailed to the cross) with a new pattern.

For many of us this is a formidable task. Even if we are able to identify these destructive patterns, they are often so ingrained in us that we find them difficult to change. This is where the good news of God's indwelling Spirit is vital. God's Word tells us that His Spirit is working within us "to will and to act according to his good purpose" (Philippians 2:13). What is His purpose? "For those God foreknew he also predestined to be *conformed to the likeness of his Son*" (Romans 8:29, emphasis added). God wants us to learn to treat people as Jesus would treat them if He were in our shoes. Our job is to partner with Him in this project, to "offer [ourselves] to Him as instruments of righteousness" (Romans 6:13) and to "continue to work out [our] salvation with fear and trembling" (Philippians 2:12).

"Fear and trembling" doesn't mean that we drive ourselves, fearful that a mean God will smite us if we fail. Rather, it means that we take seriously God's passion to see us become the loving, faithful, generous people He created us to be. It's not our job to remake ourselves. It's our job to make our hearts available to God for restoration. Paul told the Ephesians that God "is able to do immeasurably more than all we ask or imagine, according to his power that is at work within us" (Ephesians 3:20). By taking time to yield ourselves to His greater power working within us, we all can change and become more like Jesus. He is the only One, through the indwelling work of the Holy Spirit, who can change our hearts, attitudes, and behaviors. Those changes can last if we continue to allow Him to reign in our lives. Our side of the deal is to pay attention to how we think and behave, to take time to reflect on the baggage in our hearts that underlies these thoughts and actions, to take these struggles to God in prayer, to choose to listen to what our spouse tells us, to fill our minds with a true picture of God, and to invite Him to strengthen us to think and act in new ways.

Don and I have changed many patterns over our more than twenty years of marriage. Certain things have been harder to change simply because we are both stubborn and hard-hearted at times, but as we have invited one another to speak truth, invoked the power of the Holy Spirit, and sought help from others, we have been changed for the better. "The beauty of marriage is that it confronts our selfishness and demands our service twenty-four hours a day," writes Gary Thomas.[3] Here are just a few areas that we found needed to be replaced.

Sarcasm

While Jan and I (Don) were dating, I asked her to spend Thanksgiving Day with my huge family. She still remembers that first meeting in unfamiliar territory. Everyone was happy to meet her, and we sat around the tables enjoying the feast. After dinner, several of my siblings and I played Trivial Pursuit. We're a competitive tribe, and Jan was shocked at the way we used sarcasm to intimidate our opponents. Our comments were made in fun, so until Jan pointed it out, I never thought about how those sarcastic words were unhealthy.

What makes sarcasm so destructive is that it is usually seasoned with a pinch of truth, laced with ridicule, and draped in humor. It is a passive-aggressive form of communication — that is, it gets a hostile message across indirectly. Proverbs 26:18-19 says, "Like a madman shooting firebrands or deadly arrows is a man who deceives his neighbor and says, 'I was only joking!'"

As Jan and I later prepared for marriage, we talked about how destructive sarcasm could be between us. I realized how sarcasm had become second nature to me. Because of my family background, my dry sense of humor, and my involvement in athletics, I was hardly aware how often I used sarcasm. I did some research on the etymology of the word "sarcasm" and found that it literally means to "tear or rip away flesh." Jan and I agreed before we married not to use sarcasm in our communication with each other and to hold one another accountable if we heard each other using it in our relationships with others.

At first it was hard for me to make that change, especially around my brothers and sisters. Eventually, though, I was able to see the pattern and, with Jan's help, realize when I was using sarcasm. Just paying attention helped me put a stop to it. We have honored our pact about sarcasm for over twenty years, and it has proven to be invaluable for maintaining a loving relationship and fostering direct communication.

Mind Reading

It wasn't until after we married that another faulty communication pattern came to the surface: mind reading. I (Jan) had been "trained" extensively in this art and expected no less from Don.

In my home growing up, we were expected to read minds. No one sat down and said such a thing, but it was part of the family script. If my stepdad was angry about something, we were expected to know what it was and how to fix it without ever asking or being told. I also learned some manipulative methods of dropping hints that were used to help others in the task of reading my mind. Asking directly for needs to be met was not standard practice in my home. One could provide vague information, but it was the other person's job to figure out what you wanted and needed without being forthright.

One day early in our marriage Don and I went to the beach. We had a nice day in the sun and were preparing to leave. I really wanted to go to our favorite Italian restaurant for dinner, but since I wasn't accustomed to asking for what I wanted, I did the only thing I knew to do—I dropped hints. As we packed up our things I said to Don, "Boy, I sure am hungry," to which he replied, "Yeah, I'm getting a little hungry myself." We got into the car and Don headed toward home. Calculating my words carefully, I said, "I don't think there's anything to eat at home." Don made no comment. As Don continued driving, I noticed we were approaching the street we would turn on in order to go to the restaurant. I pointed out the window and said, "There's the street we'd turn on if we were going to Mama Cozza's." "Yep, there it is," Don said in an oblivious tone. We continued on our way. By this time I was ticked! *This man does not get it!* When we finally arrived home, I went directly to the kitchen, opened the refrigerator, looked inside, and pronounced in an angry tone, "Yeah, there's nothing in here to eat." I proceeded to open several cupboard doors and slam them shut.

"Jan, what's wrong with you?" Don asked.

"I'm mad at you!" I said.

"What for?"

"Because you would not take me to our favorite Italian restaurant!"

"You didn't ask me," said Don.

Minor point! I thought.

We discussed the whole event and, with Don's help, I recognized how unhealthy and manipulative this pattern of dropping hints was. I was able to share with Don how common it was for me growing up and that I didn't want to continue it in our marriage. He encouraged me to ask him directly when there was something I wanted or needed. As he'll attest now, I have no problem asking for what I want or need!

I've talked with several couples who have the same problem. Here's the most common scenario: Husband forgets to do something. Wife gets angry and silent. Husband notices her withdrawal and asks, "What's wrong, honey?" (Most of you know what answer follows.) "Nothing," says the wife in a tone that lets her husband know he is in bigger trouble than he was before he asked. This game can go on forever. Believe me, I know, because I was an expert at it when we first married. I would tell Don nothing was wrong but punish him for days for what he didn't know.

It took some re-training of thought patterns and a change in communication skills for me to work this through. I had to realize that Don could not figure out on his own when I needed a hug after dealing with sick kids and being shut in the house all day. I had to ask him for it and not feel slighted if he didn't volunteer it on his own. I also had to learn that if you ask for something and get it, it should not be devalued. (In other words, it isn't fair to say to your spouse, "It's no good now because I had to ask for it.") It is healthy for us to share appropriate needs with our mate and have our mates respond. This builds trust and safety in a relationship.

CONFLICT RESOLUTION

It was several years into our marriage before we discovered a healthy model for resolving our conflicts. Neither of our parents modeled good conflict resolution skills, and we followed suit. Don would withdraw from conflict and avoid the issue. I would pursue and escalate until the issue got bigger than the original incident.

In counseling, I often hear two extremes: parents who "never" seemed to have any conflicts that were apparent to the children, or parents who had constant conflict that "never" got resolved and to which the children were overexposed. Both extremes can leave children feeling hopeless and inadequate when they have to solve problems in adult relationships. The former condition leaves the person with the unrealistic notion that there is something drastically wrong with his marriage because his parents "never" had conflicts. Because all relationships experience conflict, this person did not observe reality nor gain a workable model for resolution. In the latter condition, children may grow up either to avoid all conflict (so as not to "be like Mom and Dad") or to replicate the poor skills their parents modeled.

Think about your home growing up. If your parents had a conflict, what usually happened? Did either parent withdraw into silence and avoidance for days, hoping it would all blow over? Did one scream at the other and leave the room in a huff? Did they discuss any issues regularly without making headway? By observing your parents, what did you learn about how to solve your problems?

What about your own relationships as an adult? Are you carrying on some of those same patterns? How do you respond to conflict? Into which category would you place your conflict resolution skills? Are they valuable or repairable, or do they need to be totally replaced?

In their excellent book *Fighting for Your Marriage*, authors Markman, Stanley, and Blumberg provide a straightforward method of problem solving. Based upon over fifteen years of marital research, the authors found that one of the most significant factors in determining the success and satisfaction of a marriage has to do with how successfully couples resolve conflict. They outline very practical steps to thoroughly discuss the problem using a Speaker/Listener format.[4] After the problem has been discussed, the couple is encouraged to set a later date for discussing a solution. The problem solution steps include:

1. Agenda setting: Make clear what you're trying to solve. Be specific.
2. Brainstorming: Together offer solutions without evaluating or filtering. Be creative. Write all suggestions down on paper.
3. Agreement and compromise: Decide together which solution or combination of solutions you both agree to try for a specific period of time. Compromise means both partners may have to give up something in order to gain something for the relationship.
4. Follow-up: Set a time to review with each other how the "trial solution" is working out. Modify your solution if necessary, and try again.[5]

In my counseling practice, the couples who have implemented these simple, practical tools have reduced the frequency of conflict and found success at working together to find solutions.

ACTION STEP: EVALUATING PATTERNS

Now that you understand how to face and trace certain patterns, you may want to pull out your assessment results and use them to further your exploration. As you look over the categories, ask yourself what familiar patterns you exhibit. Ask your mate to share with you what he or she observes. Are these patterns valuable, repairable, or replaceable? It may help to list them in columns for future reference.

WHAT'S NEXT?

You may have discovered that facing and tracing your history are useful tools in understanding yourself and your mate. You've assessed the damage and determined what needs repair and replacement. The next tool helps to give you access to the Holy Spirit's power to genuinely erase faulty patterns. It helps you lighten your load by removing excess baggage. What is this miraculous tool? It is called reconciliation.

CHAPTER 7

RECONCILING YOUR HISTORY

ERASING

BEFORE DON AND I MARRIED, NEITHER OF US MADE A habit of reconciling our checkbooks. It wasn't until six years ago that this changed. My friend Lauren told me about a software program that might ease our pain when it came to tax time. Lauren graciously came to our home and spent hours setting up the software and plugging in our account information. We now have most of our financial records on computer.

Part of what prompted this was the horrific days leading up to our tax appointment each year. I still hate every minute of the preparation and loathe sitting with our accountant. Don't get me wrong—she is a very nice lady and does an excellent job. But I can't think of anything that I dislike more than finding out about what we paid, what we owe, and what next year will require!

The only pleasure I seem to get from working on our finances is reconciling our statements on computer. Each month I turn on our computer, open our Quicken software, click on the "reconcile" button, open my bank statement, and begin. I check off all deposits, review checks and their amounts, and watch the bottom line, hoping it will read "0.00." When it does, I get to my favorite part. The screen asks me to indicate by clicking on the "finished" box or the "finish later" box. If the bottom line reads "0.00" and I click on the finished box, I see what I've been waiting for! A new screen opens with a large graphic of a bright yellow sunrise. Emblazoned across the top of the sun's rays is the word *Congratulations!* Below the sunrise is a moneybag with a large dollar sign, which seems to assume you have some money left to be happy about. To the left it says, "Your account is balanced. The items you have marked have been reconciled in your register."

I'm not sure why I feel such satisfaction when I see that congratulations sunshine each month. Were it accurate, the moneybag would have a cent sign on it with a hole in the bottom, signaling the software user that whatever pittance is left will be trickled away when the program is reopened the following month. Still, I get a warm feeling inside knowing that the reconciliation is complete.

What does the word *reconcile* conjure up in your mind? Do you think of it in terms of balancing or bringing together things that were at odds? Does it make you think of setting things straight? Of resolving differences? We're going to look at four areas where reconciliation is needed: first, with God; second, with our family of origin; third, with others; fourth, with our mate.

But before we look at those specific relationships, let's consider what reconciling your history means and how it relates to *erasing.*

CANCELING THE DEBT

Reconciling your history is the process of bringing your past to harmony and resolution. It lightens your load of hurts. In spiritual terms, reconciliation is about forgiveness. God's forgiveness and grace at work in our lives gives us a new start, a chance to free ourselves from the burdens of the past.

Colossians 2:13-14 (MSG) puts it this way:

> When you were stuck in your old sin-dead life, you were incapable of responding to God. God brought you alive— right along with Christ! Think of it! All sins forgiven, the slate wiped clean, that old arrest warrant canceled and nailed to Christ's Cross.

When we're reconciled, it means that a debt has been canceled and we're free to live without the burden of it. Don and I call this "lighthearted living." It's living free from the weights of our past. Reconciliation doesn't mean that we erase the past; it means that we bring the past to God, who is the Reconciler. He is the One who cancels the debt our history has incurred. Through the process Don and I are describing in this book, He redeems our history for His glory. He helps us erase the negative *effects* of our past by transforming us in the present.

Reconciliation is something God initiates and continues to interweave in our lives.

RECONCILED TO GOD

In order for us to travel lighter, we must first be reconciled to God. In 2 Corinthians 5:17-19, Paul tells us that God is the author of our reconciliation, and that through Christ He has given us the ministry of reconciliation:

> Therefore, if anyone is in Christ, he is a new creation; the old has gone, the new has come! All this is from God, who

> reconciled us to himself through Christ and gave us the min-
> istry of reconciliation: that God was reconciling the world to
> himself in Christ, not counting men's sins against them. And
> he has committed to us the message of reconciliation.

Reconciliation is something God accomplishes, exercising His grace toward sinful humans.[1] God initiates the process and brings it to completion. He exchanges our sinfulness with Christ's righteousness because Christ paid the price for our sin and we have been declared free from the penalty.

What this means in practical terms is that when we have accepted Christ as our Lord and Savior by faith, we have a "0.00" balance. We are forever reconciled to God, with nothing left unaccounted for. We can have the rich satisfaction of knowing we have been reconciled through our faith in what Jesus did on our behalf. This is true freedom! God has poured out His grace to us, not on the basis of our actions or worthiness, but solely on the basis of "His righteousness credited to my account because of my faith in Him."[2]

I must confess that this truth has been difficult for me to truly grasp. Although I have been a Christian for thirty-seven years, I grew up in a church and home environment that talked grace but lived law. Even as a young elementary student in Sunday school, I figured out that the rewards came to those who memorized verses, did their lessons, and could recite the books of the Bible flawlessly. I heard my Sunday school teacher and pastor teach about grace as God's gift, based on faith not on works — but performance earned the attention and gold stars! It has taken me years to root out that performance-oriented belief system that was so deeply embedded into the soil of my life.

For many of us, the history of our experience is not easily

overcome. We may have grown up hearing one thing but experiencing something drastically different. The result often is a split between what our head knows is truth and what our heart believes. Dr. David Scamands writes extensively about this. As a pastor, seminary professor, and missionary, he says,

> *"It is surprising the number of genuine Christians who are caught in an inner conflict between what they think about God and what they feel about God (and how He feels toward them). . . . Regardless of how much correct doctrine Christians may know, until they have a picture and a felt sense that God is truly good and gracious, there can be no lasting spiritual victory in their lives."*[3]

Being reconciled to God involves integrating the truth in our heads with the belief in our hearts. Most of us will never fully integrate these truths this side of eternity. But we can echo Paul's prayer in Ephesians when he prayed that we "may have power, together with all the saints, to grasp how wide and long and high and deep is the love of Christ, and to *know* this love that surpasses knowledge — that [we] may be filled to the measure of all the fullness of God" (Ephesians 3:18-19, emphasis added). The word *know* here means to understand completely. It implies relationship.[4] In other words, it is not an abstract, distant knowing, but a deep, up-close-and-personal knowing.

John Townsend and Henry Cloud write about the discrepancy between head and heart in their book *How People Grow.*

> *[Some people] "know" the information in their heads, but they are far from "knowing" it in their hearts. They*

commonly think this "head" knowledge is somehow going to
"sink in" to their hearts. This is not the way things work.
The head and the heart work in different ways. The head
works with "information gathering," the heart works with
"experience gathering."[5]

The authors add that it is *experiencing* God's love in the context of relationship that helps us grow.

Your concept of God is largely shaped by your experience in your family. If you grew up with a dad who was affirming, attentive, and encouraging, you most likely will have little trouble relating to God as a loving and caring Father. If, however, your dad was absent, abusive, or critical, you will experience some ambivalence in relating to God as a Father who is full of lovingkindness toward you. You may know the truth in your head, but your heart may remain distant or cautious as you approach God as Father.

I had been a Christian for several years before I realized how I had transferred the image of my earthly father to my heavenly Father. Because my history included an abandoning and abusive father, it was difficult to relate to God on anything other than those terms. It wasn't that I didn't *know* the truth in my head — I did. I could quote verses about the love of God and expound truths about His character from Scripture. But my heart was not fully reconciled to God because of my experience.

This may be true for you as well. If it is, please know that God understands this and is not put off by your mistrust. He knows where it has come from, and He wants to reconcile you and your history to Himself. He usually does not do this in one sweeping wave of His hand. Rather, He patiently rebuilds your experience through a process of time, just as a child learns to trust. Your part is to recognize that there are areas of your heart that may not be fully reconciled to His truth and to ask Him to bring those issues into harmony with Him as you walk with Him day by day.

Several years ago when our daughters were very young, I opened my heart to the Lord about my hurt over never knowing the genuine love of a daddy. My biological father left when I was five, and my stepfather's abuse of me began at age seven. As an adult at thirty-three years old, I cried out to God, "Please, Lord, show me your Daddy's heart of love." Three weeks went by and I had forgotten my prayer, but the Lord had not. While sitting in our den one evening, I was watching Don with our daughters in the living room. Our oldest daughter, Heather, left the room and came back with two pillows. The first she put under her dad's head and the other one she laid right next to him on the floor. She lay down and snuggled in close. Our younger daughter, Kellie, then picked up her favorite blanket and placed it on Don's chest and laid her head sweetly down. As I watched this tender scene, Don looked up at me with a huge grin on his face, as if to say, "These are my precious girls in whom my heart delights." At that instant, I heard the Spirit of God speak in my innermost being and say, "Jan, *that* is my Daddy's heart of love for you." At that moment, there was a reconciling of my history that no one other than God, who transcends time, could accomplish in the heart of a woman who desperately longed to know a Father's love. God has been so faithful to me in His love over the years. He continues to reconcile my heart and head to be congruent in my knowledge of Him. He uses His Word, other people, my experience, and His Spirit to accomplish this.

One of the most tragic results of sin in our world has less to do with what happens to us and more to do with what happens to our understanding of God as a result of events in our history. During my recovery from sexual abuse I struggled with why God did not intervene in my life to prevent the abuse. I wrestled with anger and questions about God's goodness. It took time to find peace in my heart and to reconcile His goodness with the events of my life. God lovingly revealed that He knows the end from the beginning. He saw what I could not see — a plan for a hope and a future. It took faith to believe Him.

Many who have suffered at the hands of someone else wonder why a loving, all-powerful God did not prevent the parent from abusing us, the spouse from betraying us, or the car accident that left us childless. I have sat with hundreds of people over the last twenty years, comforting many who have been disillusioned and angry with God over His apparent indifference. Yet He has a redemptive plan — and He longs for us to experience it.

I don't know what your history has been or what experiences have helped shape you. But I do know with my whole heart that God wants to meet you in your need. He wants to resolve and bring to harmony what has been lost through the sin and brokenness of your past. He is waiting to do so — will you let Him?

Pause right now and pray this simple prayer:

> Lord, I'm not sure what all needs to be reconciled to You,
> but I want to allow you to have full access to my life. I want
> to have a relationship with You that is not just based out of
> my head, but one that flows also from my heart. Please
> remove the obstacles, the distortions, and the belief systems

*rooted in my past that prevent me from fully knowing You
and Your love for me. In Jesus' name, amen.*

If you prayed that prayer, God will meet you where you are.
The apostle Paul wrote this encouragement to the believers in
Rome:

> *You see, at just the right time, when we were still powerless,
> Christ died for the ungodly. Very rarely will anyone die for a
> righteous man, though for a good man someone might possi-
> bly dare to die. But God demonstrates his own love for us in
> this: While we were still sinners, Christ died for us. . . . For
> if, when we were God's enemies, we were reconciled to him
> through the death of his Son, how much more, having been
> reconciled, shall we be saved through his life!*
> *(Romans 5: 6-8,10)*

You can be assured that God is working out that reconciliation in your life right now. Through His love and forgiveness, you
have been set free. Because of this freedom, you have been given
the "ministry of reconciliation," which is the message of forgiveness — for your family, for others, and for your mate.

RECONCILED TO YOUR FAMILY OF ORIGIN

We've talked extensively about the importance of your history
and how that history plays itself out in your relationships. You've
faced your historical baggage, and through tracing, you've seen
how your history repeats itself if you are not intentional about
changing certain patterns. You're ready to begin the process of
erasing through reconciling your relationships.

To be reconciled to your family of origin means that unresolved issues, hurts, disappointments, or fractures need to be resolved. How do you do this? Sometimes you need the assistance of a professional who can help you sort out your feelings and the events that have shaped you. But, ultimately, resolution involves forgiveness.

> Forgiveness, like many other areas in our Christian life, is a process. It may be that you can truly and totally forgive your husband for making an unkind statement a minute after he makes it. For some it takes longer. The deeper the wound inflicted, the longer the process of forgiveness. This doesn't mean that you are given license to hold onto bitterness, anger, and resentment. It does mean that the more serious the injury inflicted, the longer it may take to work through the emotions toward the final goal of forgiveness.[6]

About five years ago, the Lord put on my heart that I was to take my stepfather out to lunch for Father's Day. Although we had a peaceable relationship, I struggled in prayer, asking the Lord why I was the one who often extended love to him, when he was the one who had ravaged my life. For days I told the Lord I didn't think I could do it. I felt ashamed for feeling this way and began doubting the forgiveness God had genuinely worked in my heart. I cried most of the way to my parents' home and on the way asked the Lord again why He wanted me to do this. I heard Him clearly say, "I have a blessing in it for you."

As my stepfather and I sat across the table over lunch, there was a bit of awkwardness, but I felt assured of the Lord's presence. In the back of my mind I thought the "blessing" God had in store for me was something that my stepdad might say to affirm me in some way. I was wrong. I was totally unprepared for the blessing God had for me. Toward the end of our lunch, with tears running down my stepfather's face, he said, "Thank you so much for taking me out to lunch — you don't know how much this has meant to me." Just then, a rush of compassion and grace flooded my heart. As I looked at my stepdad, I saw a broken man who desperately needed the mercy of God in his life. The blessing was that God gave *me* that mercy for *him*, again. As I looked at him, I didn't see the man who had abused me for eleven years — I saw a man needing the love of a Savior who died for us all. As I drove home, the Lord reminded me that one of the greatest blessings is that of giving grace to one who is undeserving. I thanked Him all the way home for His grace in my life.

RECONCILED TO OTHERS

It is all too common that marriage partners bring relational baggage into their marriage from past relationships. The baggage may come from romantic relationships, previous marriages, or friendships that have some unresolved or unhealthy roots. If we apply the definition of reconciliation, then it is important for us to resolve issues that have the potential to pull us away from or disturb the harmony of our marital relationship.

In counseling couples, I've discovered four warning signs that indicate relational reconciliation is needed. If either you or your mate persistently engage in one of the following, you may need assistance in reconciling your history:

- fantasizing about another person (past or present)
- comparing your mate with another person (past or present)

- longing for contact or connection with another person (past or present)
- reacting to your mate on the basis of your relationship to another person (past or present)

In most instances, the need for reconciliation with others revolves around emotional ties. Emotional ties are sometimes referred to as "soul ties." They are feelings of attachment that have not been properly dealt with. They may be the result of romantic attachment or injury attachment. If not responded to appropriately, these ties deplete and distract a couple's ability to bond together.

Romantic Attachment

What do you do with feelings of affection or attachment that remain after you marry? First of all, you need to be honest about them. Honesty in this situation does not mean full disclosure with your mate. It means you recognize that the feelings are there and understand that they may be there for a variety of reasons. You cannot always sort out the reasons yourself, so it can be helpful to seek outside guidance. Wise counsel can protect you from making a life-altering decision (such as divorce) solely based on your "affections."

Tammi came into counseling for marital issues. She had been happily married to Carl for eleven years, but lately she was feeling dissatisfied in their relationship. She'd recently connected with friends from college and discovered they shared a mutual acquaintance. She and that mutual acquaintance, Steve, had been friends in high school, but she had not seen him since. Tammi's friends invited Carl and her to dinner, and she was pleasantly surprised to see Steve there. She and Steve laughed about the time in chemistry class when Steve rescued her from the Bunsen burner that almost caught her hair on fire. They talked off and on that evening, and Tammi remembered how easy it was to talk to Steve. She wondered why they had not stayed connected.

For days after the dinner, she found herself reminiscing about Steve's easy-going personality. She couldn't believe he was divorced — who wouldn't want to be with such a great guy? After a few weeks, she pulled out her yearbook one afternoon to read what Steve had written. He had talked about being "friends for life."

Tammi began wondering what life would have been like had she married Steve rather than Carl. Anytime she and Carl had a conflict, her mind ran wild with thoughts about how Steve would handle the situation so much differently than Carl. Tammi felt guilty about her constant comparing, but she wondered if she'd made the wrong decision by marrying Carl. She came in for counseling to try to sort out her feelings.

Tammi was caught up in both fantasizing and comparing. Many of us have fleeting thoughts about what our lives might be like if we had chosen another mate, career, or life path. Tammi's "obsession" had to do with what she was longing for in her marriage and the emotional attachment that had not been laid to rest with Steve. Fortunately, Tammi did not pursue a relationship with Steve, although many people are drawn into this snare. Through counseling she recognized her need to give up the emotional tie to Steve. She had to refuse to feed her fantasies, and redirect her focus and affections. This discovery opened the door of understanding for her and eventually led to a deeper relationship with her husband as they worked to create intimacy in areas that were underdeveloped in their marriage.

Emotional ties such as these need to be severed or laid to rest. Sometimes there are underlying issues of a historical nature that drive these ties, so it's helpful to explore them with a counselor, but it is never beneficial to feed such affections. If you are aware of emotional ties with someone other than your mate, ask God to sever those ties. You may need to sit down with the Lord and confess any fantasies or preoccupation of thought about that person, or you may need to express feelings still bound up with that person. Ask God to sever all those ties and to redirect the energy, emotions, and thoughts into a richer, healthier love for your mate. If you find you resist this idea because you enjoy those thoughts, this discussion should be a warning to you. Remember that "As [a man] thinketh in his heart, so is he" (Proverbs 23:7, KJV). If you continue to meditate on or muse over attachments outside of your marriage, you will find yourself crossing a line that will bring only heartache.

INJURY ATTACHMENT

Early in our marriage I was jealous and distrustful. One day after Don came home from work, he walked in the bedroom as I was going through his pants pockets. He asked what I was doing. I told him I was looking for evidence. He was stunned as I told him of my concern that he might be unfaithful to me. He put his arms around me and said, "Jan, you can trust me."

I then sobbed in his arms. "I want to trust you, but you don't understand. Every man in my past, with one exception, has betrayed me. It's hard for me not to expect the same from you." Don looked me in the eyes and said, "Honey, I love you. You can trust me, but if you continue to expect me to betray you, I will probably fall prey to your expectations. If you will trust me, I will not let you down." I remember throwing myself on our bed and crying out to the Lord. Everything in me desperately wanted to trust Don, but another part of me grasped for self-protection — *if you trust him and then he lets you down, then what?* I realized that the wounds from past betrayals were oozing out like poisonous toxins into my heart. The unresolved hurt prevented me from embracing Don's love and commitment to me. I prayed, "Lord, you know how hard this is for me. I want to trust Don with all my heart, but I am so afraid he will betray me like so many of the men in my life. Please, Lord, help me to let go of my past and all the lies I've believed about men, so that I might love and trust my husband."

Something changed in my heart that day. I had to reconcile my history of past betrayals before God and relinquish my self-protection. I had to forgive those who had betrayed me and refuse to let my history determine my future. "Forgiveness . . . is an act of self-defense, a tourniquet that stops the fatal bleeding of resentment."[7]

God's forgiveness covers all sin — the sin committed against us as well as the sin we commit ourselves. This truth came flooding into my heart through the words of this worship chorus:

At the Cross . . . (echo)
Where the wrongs I have done,
And the wrongs done to me —
Were nailed there with Him,
There at the Cross.

On that day, in an instant I saw in my mind's eye all the injustices, betrayals, injuries, acts of commission and omission in my life — all were nailed to the Cross. I saw Jesus hanging there, in complete submission, dying my death for me, so that I might have life and freedom. Tears streamed down my face as I realized how often I had let my own sins and the sins of others rob me of this great truth. His sacrifice was enough. His grace is sufficient.

When we have been wounded in past relationships, we need healing. For some, this healing may require professional assistance, depending on the severity of the injury. For others, the recognition of the injury coupled with an opportunity to share and work through the emotions provide the initial steps necessary for the healing to occur. For all, healing means opening our hearts to God, giving Him full access to the wounds, and forgiving. If you have been injured, ask God to mend your heart. He is able to heal your wounds and restore you to whole-ness and freedom.

RECONCILED TO YOUR MATE

Reconciling your history as it relates to your mate means that you bring to harmony, settle, or resolve your past together so that it does not continue to drain your marital bank account.

Issues from your dating life, early marriage, or even yesterday need to be resolved so that they don't pull on your relationship now or in the future. Unresolved anger and hurt grow from day to day. Like ravenous birds, they feed themselves without restraint. That is why Paul admonishes us, "Do not let the sun go down while you are still angry" (Ephesians 4:26).

I'm surprised at how many couples don't know some simple guidelines about how to be reconciled with one another. Some simple steps may help. First, hear one another out. Each of you should take time to listen and paraphrase back to your mate what he or she has told you about the issue at hand. After making sure *both* of you feel heard and understood, you each ask forgiveness for your part in the misunderstanding and release each other from the debt.

Many couples who come in for counseling have never looked at their mate, owned personal responsibility for something, and said the words, "I was wrong. I'm sorry. Would you forgive me?" I make couples practice this in session. It is humbling, but necessary.

When a conflict arises, both partners have usually contributed in some way. It is rare that one mate is fully in the right and the other fully in the wrong. In most cases, we each have some responsibility for the interaction or response to the interaction. There's a short verse in 1 John that is often understood in a global sense regarding our sin, but one day I realized how applicable it is to marital issues. It says: "If we claim to be without sin, we deceive ourselves and the truth is not in us" (1 John 1:8).

Most of us, as Christians, would never claim to be "without sin" before God in a larger context, because we know we're sinners saved by grace. But how often in relational issues with our mates do we claim to be without sin! I see it all the time — not just in my office, but when I look in the mirror. Sometimes I justify my position by ranting to myself about how Don is totally wrong on "this one" and I am right. It usually doesn't take long before the Holy Spirit quickens this verse to my heart, reminding me that in virtually any given situation I have sin to claim as my own — even if it is only in the realm of my attitude.

At a marriage retreat sponsored by our church, a couple who had been married forty years shared their story. Harriet shared how, for the first sixteen years of their marriage, she was inappropriately tied in to pleasing her mother. She talked about how on many occasions she catered more to her mother than she did to her husband and their growing family. She finally realized her unhealthy attachment and went to her husband, Paul, and asked forgiveness for the lost years in their relationship. Paul stood up and shared how, for the next nineteen years of their marriage, he remained angry and resentful, punishing Harriet for the previous sixteen years. He then looked around the room and said, "We wasted thirty-five years. It's only been in the last five years that we've come to know how to live and love each other. Don't *you* make the same mistake." Both of them, now in their seventies, learned what it means to be reconciled.

What about you? Are you wasting time being resentful or bitter? Have you refused to forgive your mate because of some injustice that occurred ten years ago — or something that happened yesterday? It is never too late to be reconciled.

RECONCILED FOR LIFE

We've talked about the need for reconciling your history in relation to God, your family of origin, others, and your mate. Reconciling is a continual process of forgiveness throughout your life. We don't wake up one day and say, "I've finally arrived! There's no more need for reconciliation." The truth is, as long as we are living and breathing, God's redemptive work of reconciliation continues. So does our need to be reconciled with others, as we daily create a history that often requires the ministry of reconciliation. Don't wait for others to do what God has called you to do. Be reconciled and erase through forgiveness the debt that was owed.

ACTION STEP: ADMITTING AND FORGIVING

Sometimes in a marriage one partner has difficulty admitting when he or she is wrong and then asking for forgiveness, while the other has difficulty forgiving because he or she tends to hold on to anger or harbor grievances. Which pattern is most typical of you?

If you have trouble humbling yourself and asking for forgiveness, meditate on James 5:16. Ask God to help you develop humility. Make it a point this week to go to your mate and admit when you've been wrong in your response, attitude, or behavior. Confess this without defensiveness and ask for your mate's forgiveness.

If you have trouble letting go of your hurt or anger and you find yourself harboring unforgiveness, meditate on Colossians 3:13. Ask God to help you forgive your mate as God has forgiven you—completely and without reserve. During the week, take opportunities to forgive your mate for irritations. You may or may not need to go to your mate. Sometimes those who have difficulty forgiving need to do so without drawing attention to the hurt, learning to let go and bear with their mate.

However, certain deeper injuries (such as infidelity, pornography use, or repetitive patterns) often require assistance and outside intervention to complete the forgiveness process. Don't expect to forgive and move on from such injuries without proper steps of accountability and godly counsel.

You have now faced your history, traced it back to its roots, and taken the necessary steps to erase the effects of your history through forgiveness. Now it is time to replace patterns that need to be changed. You can't fully release what you have not fully embraced, so you'll be challenged to claim your baggage at a deeper level. Don't turn back now—your destination of a stronger marriage is within view. Stay on board!

CHAPTER 8

CLAIMING YOUR BAGGAGE

REPLACING

YOUR HISTORY IS WOVEN FROM THE EVENTS AND EXPERI-
ences of your life. Your baggage is your *emotional response* to
your history. That emotional baggage may be claimed or
unclaimed. *Claimed baggage* is what you recognize is yours and deal
with forthrightly. What you ignore, deny, or minimize is
unclaimed.

You started the process of claiming your baggage when you
made a road map showing the bald facts of your history (chapter
2). You took the next step when you used an assessment to *face*
some present harmful behaviors (chapter 3). You went deeper
when you *faced* ways in which you may not have left your parents
and cleaved to your spouse (chapters 4-5). You then learned how
to *trace* present behaviors to their roots in the past (chapter 6) and
how to *erase* corrosive influence of the past by reconciling yourself
to God and others (chapter 7). You're now ready for the final step:
replacing worn-out habits with better ones.

The replacing step uses the tools you've already learned,
along with three new tools, to claim your baggage at a deeper
level. Those new tools include 1. taking personal ownership,

2. grieving, and 3. returning to God. You'll find that once you've claimed your baggage at this level, you can unpack it and unload its burden from your marriage.

Claiming your baggage at a deeper level involves more than a cursory admission of ownership. So many times when counseling a couple, I hear one or both mates say, "I know I've contributed to this problem, but . . ." Deeper level claiming has no additions, no excuses, no disclaimers, and no justifications. It is a straightforward confession of owning what is yours and a genuine commitment to cooperate with God toward change. Confession and cooperation are not always easy, especially when they touch an intimate relationship.

WHAT'S IN YOUR OVERNIGHT BAG?

The early years of our marriage confronted us with the differences that most couples face with regard to sex. Men and women are "wired" differently and approach the sexual relationship uniquely. There are numerous excellent books that help couples with these issues. Don and I needed to educate ourselves about those differences, but we carried additional baggage, too. We've used the following analogy in our seminars to help couples understand what it's like when your history follows you into the bedroom.

Picture a man in a wheelchair. He has been confined to the chair all of his life. From the moment he rises in the morning until he is assisted to bed every evening, he remains in that chair. After all these years, it has become a part of his identity. In fact, he feels lost without it except for once a week, the day he keeps his established appointment for physical therapy. The therapy places him in a warm, bubbling whirlpool for an hour. The man can hardly wait to get there each week. It's the only time he gets out of the confinement of that wheelchair. It's a time when he can feel freedom and pleasure. He gets to "let loose." He dreams about the whirlpool between appointments, and on the day of the appointment he wakes up with excitement.

Now picture a five-year-old girl. Her father is a harsh man with a military background. He has trained many soldiers, and he runs his home the same way. He was an athlete in school and an excellent swimmer. He decides one day that it's time for the girl to learn to swim. He does not sign her up in a local swimming class, but decides to expose her to the water himself. He marches her to the backyard, where the family whirlpool is. Without warning, he throws her in.

She cannot swim, nor can she touch bottom. She comes up for air only to hear her father say, "You're all right; just a few more minutes." Then he shoves her head back under water. She is terrified that she will die.

When she finally gets out of the whirlpool, she never wants to go near the water again. She lives in constant fear that she may not survive her next "swimming lesson."

Now that you have the man in the wheelchair and the little girl firmly pictured in your mind, imagine that they marry each other. The whirlpool represents the sexual relationship. The man in the wheelchair is Don, and I am the little girl.

All his life, Don was confined to a world without feelings or affection. He was restricted and restrained. He goes to the whirlpool with expectation and eagerness. The whirlpool is the only place he feels unhindered and free. He can experience and express emotions there unlike any other place he has ever been. He longs for this freedom and pursues it with intensity.

I am the little girl who was thrown into adult sexual intimacy without warning. I was not prepared for the terror, helplessness, and confusion. It's no wonder that I fear the whirlpool and all it represents. Even though the whirlpool has changed locations, it is fraught with reminders that are not easily erased.

We use this analogy to illustrate how our history has influenced our perspectives. In the beginning of our marriage, the man in the wheelchair approached the little girl saying, "All right! Just what I've been waiting for! Let's you and me go to the whirlpool!"

"Oh no!" the little girl shrieked in horror. "Not the whirlpool!"

Which perspective is right—that of the man in the wheelchair or that of the little girl? There is neither a right or wrong perspective; both are valid in light of their different points of reference. We had to learn this about each other and have compassion for each other before we could move through our histories to develop a healthy history of our own.

The good news is that perspectives can change as we gather new information and embrace new experiences. The man in the wheelchair has learned how to be less obsessive about going to the whirlpool by developing other areas where he can get out of the confinement of his chair and experience freedom. The girl has learned to trust the man in the wheelchair not to force her head under water and to enjoy the tender moments of relaxation and fulfillment that come from being in the whirlpool together.

In practical terms, sometimes the man in the wheelchair gently approaches the little girl, asking her to climb up into his lap so he might hug and cuddle her while they sit by the whirlpool. He waits until the fear leaves her eyes and asks, "Do you think we can stick our feet in yet?"

"Yes, I think so, but let's take it slowly," warns the little girl.

Over time, the warmth of the man's love and the tenderness of his caring touch calm the little girl's fears. She transitions from the little girl to a woman who longs to unite with the man she loves and embrace together God's complete design for a husband and wife.

Don't think that this happened overnight! This was a process—and through walking this process together we grew more intimate and more in love. We learned some valuable lessons about leaving our baggage behind. We had to take personal ownership of our baggage at a deeper level, grieve through our losses, and wholeheartedly turn to God for help.

WHO'S RESPONSIBLE NOW?

Most of us have a bag or two of hurts and injustices. They contain our responses to others' mistakes, influences, or oversights. We surveyed that baggage in chapter 2 when we discussed obvious and obscure losses. You may have discovered that your losses have affected you much more than you knew. You're now at a crossroads because as an adult, you are responsible for what you do with your history. Others are responsible for what they did then; you are responsible for what you do now. What you do today with your past will shape your future.

An illustration may help you distinguish others' responsibility from your own. When we purchased our home nine years ago, I was excited about the built-in gas barbeque in the backyard. I envisioned regularly having people over to enjoy food and fellowship on our patio. For eight years, my vision was reality.

Last year we noticed that the tile countertop around the barbeque had cracked in spots and caved in. The brick encasement that housed the barbeque remained intact. I called a repairman for an estimate. He took one look at the tile and said, "I can't believe they put this tile out here."

I asked, "What do you mean?"

"Whoever installed this used the extra tile from the interior of your home, not tile suited for outside surfaces."

This should have been a clue to what would follow. We discussed the repair options and decided to match the existing brick rather than replacing the tile.

I hired a bricklayer. He removed the tile and called me out to see the hollowed pit. Inside was debris left behind by the builders: broken tile, dirt, a plastic cup from McDonalds, shards of cement, nails, trash, and a beer can.

"They used this as a dumping ground instead of hauling it away. We'll take care of it. We have to clean it out before we can rebuild the frame." He pointed to some wood inside the encasement and said, "See this? The wood is rotted and scorched. But that's not the biggest problem."

I shut my eyes and braced myself. "Do you see that copper tubing? Whoever put in this barbeque used copper tubing to run the gas line. That's illegal. I can't hook up your new unit because this is not up to code. You'll have to hire someone to replace this."

I sighed. "What will that entail? Who do I call?"

"You'll need a plumber. It looks like he'll have to dig a trench to the gas line. Do you know where your shutoff valve is?"

I led him over to the valve on the side of our house. He took one look at it and said, "Looks like you'll need someone to do some cement work too. I bet the line runs under this cement slab, so that will have to be broken up and replaced as well."

I thought I was having a nightmare. One thing had led to

another and then another and another. Would this ever end?

He offered one more thought. "You know, since this copper tubing was installed illegally, you might want to go back to the builder and make them pay for it. They knew it wasn't legal to do it this way. They just took the easy way out. You're lucky you didn't have an explosion."

I went to work. I got my camera and took several snapshots of the encasement and the copper tubing. I phoned the builder but found that another company had bought them out. After further research I discovered that the current company technically was still liable for all work done by the original builder. It was suggested that I go to the city planning department to obtain copies of the original building permits. I was told that the builders probably had not obtained a permit for the barbeque because they knew it would never have passed inspection. I wrote a letter describing in detail what had happened, enclosed the pictures, and asked the company to pay half the cost of repair. I explained my position as a homeowner who purchased the property in good faith, assuming it was up to legal building standards. I received a letter back that said they had no intention of paying. Their liability on defects was limited to ten years, and sixteen years had elapsed.

I was indignant and called a friend who was an attorney. He said I could pursue the case legally, but I would have to show evidence that the original company neglected to install the proper gas line and that they had "an intent to defraud" the homeowner. My friend said, "Jan, you could pursue this. It seems that because they did not obtain the proper permit, they knew they were wrong — but it's difficult to prove intent to defraud."

It's hard for me to admit defeat, but I realized I was at the end.

At some level, I knew an injustice had been done and that the responsible party should take ownership. On another level, I knew that too many years had passed. The truth was, we had purchased this home, lived in it comfortably, enjoyed the benefits, welcomed friends and family into it, and successfully weathered previous repairs and difficulties that are always a part of home ownership. I realized I had several options. I could be angry, go to court, and demand payment. I could be angry and never have the barbeque repaired as a statement to the world that it was not my fault. I could be depressed, have it fixed, and let it gnaw at me every time I threw a hamburger on the grill. Or I could let it go. I could accept what had happened, take responsibility to repair it, and enjoy the benefits that would make up the future. It was up to me.

In your marriage, you are faced with similar challenges. You can look into your history and the internal workings of your marriage and determine that injustices were done. You can spend time, energy, and emotion compiling evidence against those who perpetrated such hurtful deeds. You can be depressed and sit around feeling victimized by what has cost you dearly. You can spend years fighting over the wrongs and consume a lifetime with bitterness and lack of forgiveness. Or you can accept what happened, take responsibility to repair it, and enjoy the benefits for years to come.

There was no doubt that the struggles Don and I faced in our intimate life had carried over from our histories. But we had a choice — and so do you. Claiming our baggage requires ownership at a deep level. It means we fully embrace our history as our own and then replace the patterns we adopted with healthier ones. We learned this in part from a man named Nehemiah.

PERSONAL OWNERSHIP AND CONFESSION

In chapter 2 we briefly discussed Nehemiah and his burden to rebuild the wall in Jerusalem. We saw how he surveyed the loss before he set about to rebuild. But what caused him to take on such a project in the first place? He hadn't caused the damage. Why would he embrace such a huge responsibility?

Nehemiah's brother Hanani and some other men told Nehemiah about the condition of Jerusalem (Nehemiah 1:2). They reported that the exiles who had returned were "in great trouble and disgrace" (1:3). Nehemiah responded with a prayer in which he took personal ownership of the problem, grieved the losses, and returned wholeheartedly to God. Here's the first part of his prayer:

> O LORD, God of heaven, the great and awesome God, who keeps his covenant of love with those who love him and obey his commands, let your ear be attentive and your eyes open to hear the prayer your servant is praying before you day and night for your servants, the people of Israel. I confess *the sins we Israelites,* including myself and my father's house, *have committed against you. We have acted wickedly toward you. We have not obeyed the commands, decrees and laws you gave your servant Moses.* (Nehemiah 1: 5-7, emphasis added)

Nehemiah took personal ownership of a problem for which he was not directly responsible and solicited God's grace for restoration. He didn't point the finger at those in past generations as the culprits for his current condition, but took personal responsibility for where he found himself. He acknowledged their sin as no different from his own. In essence, he was saying to God, "They did these things, but so do I!"

Nehemiah did not claim to be more righteous than others. He took responsibility for his own sin and the sins of his "father's house," his extended family for many generations. He was not saying he was responsible for all his family's sins, but he was saying that his sin, as well as the sin of Israel, could be placed in the same category — it was all committed against God. Likewise, you and I and our families are all on level ground when it comes to sin. We all fall short of the glory of God (Romans 3:23).

So often, I encounter couples who are stuck in the blame game with each other. They are clueless about their own sin but experts on the ways in which their partner falls short. They've settled into styles of relating and have grown accustomed to unhealthy habits. They choose to remain stuck in sinful patterns with their mates rather than do the hard work of change.

This was true of Ben and Rachel. They'd been married over thirty years and had four grown children. They both worked in the medical field and shared some common interests. They'd attended the same church for many years and had served alongside one another. On the surface their marriage looked good, but behind closed doors it was a different story.

Ben was a pleaser who'd spent their entire marriage trying to make Rachel happy. He catered to her wishes at his own expense, telling himself he loved her sacrificially. When angry, he would withdraw into computer games and refuse to talk in order to get back at Rachel for her control. On the outside, Ben looked like the nice guy who would do anything to please his wife. On the inside, he was full of anger and resentment. He hated Rachel's long list of demands and her constant ridicule, but he suffered in silence, determined to be the martyr.

Rachel was stuck initially as well. She thought that if Ben would just spend more time with her, she would be happy. But when Ben did spend more time with her, she wanted something else. They created a habitual cycle of Rachel's demands and Ben's compliance. This pattern went on for over twenty-five years.

Finally, Rachel sought help. She realized that she was miserable and that their marriage was in trouble. She admitted that she was everything that Ben had accused her of being. She was controlling, critical, jealous, selfish, and insecure. But she had something that Ben didn't have: humility. She and Ben came in for counseling, but it wasn't long until Ben quit. For the first several weeks, we focused on Rachel's controlling behavior, and Ben sat smugly on the couch. When we started addressing Ben's anger and his withdrawal from the marriage, he was anything but receptive. He insisted that Rachel was to blame for everything in their marriage. He defended himself by saying he was a good man who got along with everyone but her. What Ben didn't see was how stuck he was in his anger. No matter how much Rachel improved, he was invested in blaming her while he maintained his golden-boy image. Even though Ben didn't come around, things changed in their marriage. How did that happen? Rachel took responsibility for changing herself.

Change in any marriage begins with one person. Take responsibility for yourself and your part in the marriage. "We need to take responsibility for our hearts, our loves, our time, and our talents. We are to own our lives and live in God's light, growing up and maturing our character along the way. . . . This is our job, and no one else's."[1]

In practical terms, taking ownership means you take your eyes off what your spouse is doing and pay more attention to how you're living and relating. Sure, it's ideal if both partners are equally invested in pursuing growth, but even if you're the only one who wants to make the effort, change is possible.

"Little changes in you can lead to huge changes in the relationship," write Clifford Notarius and Howard Markman in *We Can Work It Out.* "The breakthrough comes when we realize that by making even small changes in ourselves, we can effect big, positive changes that make us more optimistic and open to our partners."[2]

Personal ownership and confession open the door to change. Grieving is the next step in moving from your former history and into a new history that will last.

GRIEVING THROUGH LOSSES

Nehemiah's first response to the news of conditions in Jerusalem was this: "When I heard these things, I sat down and wept. For some days I mourned and fasted and prayed before the God of heaven" (Nehemiah 1:4).

Nehemiah grieved. His first response wasn't anger over injustice, nor vengeance against those who destroyed the city, nor a victimized hopelessness and despair. His first response was to enter a season of grief.

I wonder what would happen if we had a similar response to broken-down marriages in our culture? I'm not just talking about the divorce rate. I'm talking about the number of marriages that are in desperate need of healing. Many Christian marriages remain intact but are "in great trouble and disgrace" (Nehemiah 1:3). What if we grieved over the condition of marriages across our country, in our churches, in our neighborhoods, and even in our own homes?

Grieving is the next step toward unloading excess baggage. In grief we come to grips with realities that we would rather ignore. In this way, it becomes the avenue through which change begins. Grief is a place where we grow.

I don't know anyone who likes to suffer, do you? Yet the apostle Paul talked about knowing Christ through suffering: "I want to know Christ and the power of his resurrection and the fellowship of sharing in his sufferings, becoming like him in his death" (Philippians 3:10).

Every time you experience the loss of something precious to you, you have the opportunity to share with Christ in His suffering. Most of us want to take every opportunity to avoid suffering and work hard at doing so. Why would we want to sign up for grief?

Henry Cloud explains:

> Grief is God's way of our getting finished with the bad stuff of life. It is the process by which we "get over it," by which we "let it go." And because of that, because it is the process by which things can be "over with," it becomes the process by which we can be available for new good things. The soul is freed from painful experience and released for new, good experience.[3]

You may use a variety of coping mechanisms to hide from your history and avoid the grieving process. You may busy yourself to the point of exhaustion, you may have become a pleaser to avoid confrontation, you may avoid being hurt by telling yourself that you are self-sufficient and don't need others in your life, you may find yourself using alcohol or drugs to numb your pain, or you may overspiritualize your condition to escape responsibility. But your history is like the sediment in the bottom of a fish tank—the least bit of stirring causes it to rise and muddy the waters of your life. We've found in our own marriage that life's stirrings have a way of splashing our histories in our faces. My goal has often been to try to prevent the "stirring" when God's goal has been to help me deal with the sediment.

One of the best ways of dealing with your history so that you can get beyond it is to walk through a grieving process. Grieving is simply pouring out your heart to God and others. You may do this with a counselor, a support group, your mate, or close friends. You may journal your prayers. You may seek prayer, support, and accountability from those who've faced similar struggles. The important thing is that you allow yourself to grieve.

What does grieving look like? In our early years of struggling to regain a healthy intimate relationship, Don and I sometimes found ourselves helpless to change a pattern. The only thing we could do was cry out to God. We wept with each other and for each other. There were nights of confusion and frustration as well as nights of promise and pleasure. We each took personal responsibility for what we carried into our relationship, and we wrestled through the aftermath by grieving the losses together. Like Nehemiah, we needed a season of grief.

Although the Bible doesn't give us a detailed account of Nehemiah's grieving process, we do have a record of one of the countless prayers he must have prayed during that time of mourning. In that prayer, we find another key element to unpacking our pain.

RETURNING TO GOD

In his prayer, Nehemiah recounts God's promise to Israel and claims it for himself and his people:

Remember the instruction you gave your servant Moses, say-
ing, "If you are unfaithful, I will scatter you among the
nations, but if you return to me and obey my commands,
then even if your exiled people are at the farthest horizon, I
will gather them from there and bring them to the place I
have chosen as a dwelling for my Name." (Nehemiah 1:8-9,
emphasis added)

I love this passage! God told Israel, no matter what you've done or how far you've gone, *if* you return to Me, I will bring you home.

Even though that promise was for the nation of Israel, the New Testament extends the same promise to us today. No matter how far offtrack you are in your marriage, God will meet you and bring you out of exile if you will return to Him.

In the Old Testament, the Hebrew word for "return" is *shub* (pronounced "shoob"). It is used approximately 1,060 times, and its basic meaning is "to move back to the point of departure."[4] Sometimes I ask couples when things started going wrong in their relationship. Many couples can pinpoint a season or an event that seemed to be pivotal in their decline. We go back to that point to carry out the necessary repair that was never done, because that was the point of departure. That repair often means undergoing a process of grieving some loss in the relationship — an affair, a finan-cial setback, a major disappointment, or a breach of trust. It requires honesty, confession, and willingness to change. Once both partners have sufficiently worked through this loss and have extended and received forgiveness, the couple can move forward.

An additional meaning in Scripture of the word "return" is "to bring back home again." The prodigal son "returns" to his father's house. We, too, "return" in this sense when we agree with God and our mate that we have sinned and when we sincerely desire to turn from that way of thinking, believing, or acting and enter afresh into relationship. Returning involves a full surrender to God and His ways.

ACTION STEP: RETURNING TO GOD

You may be ready right now to claim some baggage and return to God with it. You may need to face some sinful patterns that you are stuck in. Maybe you have rationalized your behavior or have been blaming your mate rather than taking responsibility for yourself. Take a minute and ask the Lord to bring to mind where you have been wrong.

You may have become embittered and resentful over some past hurts. You may have rescued your mate once too often, preventing him or her from taking needed responsibility. You may have given in to despair because your situation seems hopeless. It's not. Agree with God about your sin.

Ask Him to forgive you, and express to Him your genuine desire to turn from the sinful pattern or attitude that is keeping you in "exile." Return wholeheartedly to God and ask for His help. Tell Him you no longer want to live life your way, but you will yield to His plan, even if there will be some hard steps ahead. Give Him control of your life and surrender your relationship to Him. Ask Him to begin the restoration process within *you*. It makes no difference what amount of baggage you have carried with you into your marriage—God is fully able to redeem it and relieve you of its effects as you seek Him and draw upon His resources.

Claiming your baggage at a deeper level requires taking personal ownership of your history, grieving through the losses individually and as a couple, and returning to God whole-heartedly. Joel 2:12-14 speaks to what we have talked about in this chapter:

> "Even now," declares the LORD, "return to me with all your
> heart, with fasting and weeping and mourning." Rend your
> heart and not your garments. Return to the LORD your God,
> for he is gracious and compassionate, slow to anger and
> abounding in love, and he relents from sending calamity.
> Who knows? He may turn and have pity and leave behind a
> blessing.

We have experienced that blessing in our marriage, and we want that for you. Part of the blessing is experiencing how sharing your history can actually enhance your relationship.

CHAPTER 9

BUILDING INTIMACY THROUGH SHARED HISTORIES

I (DON) HAVE LIVED WITH BACK AND LEG PAIN SINCE THE age of fifteen; I injured my back playing high school football. The injury ended my football career, and I took pain medication while I played basketball in high school and college.

The summer before my senior year in college, the pain became so intense that I couldn't sit down for more than ten minutes at a time. Finally, three weeks before school started, I had back surgery. I knew the surgery was successful when I woke up and the pain was gone. I was thrilled to be active again. I had three pain-free years but reinjured my back while coaching basketball the spring before I turned twenty-five. Back and leg pain returned, and I was hospitalized for treatment. Although I wasn't feeling well, I had just accepted a head coaching job, which I began that summer.

The pain worsened. One morning I woke in intense pain but had little feeling from my waist down. I panicked. I called my friend Gary Smith, the basketball coach at the University of Redlands. Gary rushed over and drove me sixty miles to the hospital where my first surgery had been performed. Gary drove ninety miles per hour as I moaned all the way. Surgery was scheduled for later that day. When I woke up from the anesthesia, the doctors told me they were not sure how much feeling would return. I could barely comprehend those words. What would life be like? Although I regained much of the feeling in my legs and feet over the next few months, I remain 20 percent disabled by chronic numbness and nerve damage.

For the rest of the summer after my surgery, I spent most days recuperating by the beach. I worked on strengthening my legs and trying to walk. One afternoon, I saw several friends out body-surfing. The sun was hot and I wanted to get in the water, but I had no balance and little leg strength. I knew if I went in, the waves could knock me off balance and I would struggle to get up. A college buddy named Rob came over to talk. I told him about my surgery. Rob saw past my tanned skin and smile and sensed my heart. He asked, "Don, would you like some help getting in the water?" I said, "Yes!" With his arm around me, Rob slowly walked me to the water's edge and held me steady as the waves splashed over my torso. Feeling that cool water against my body was so refreshing. Experiencing such kindness was humbling.

When Jan and I were dating, I told her about my surgeries and constant pain. On the outside I looked athletic, coached basketball, taught physical education, and by all appearances seemed like the picture of health. It was difficult at that time to measure how my injury would affect us. Neither of us could envision how it would play itself out in our married life.

When Don first told me (Jan) the story about Rob, tears welled up in his eyes. No one knew the fear that had gripped his heart about the possibility of never walking again. No one knew the pain he suffered daily. But this one act of kindness by a casual friend touched him deeply. I don't think Rob knew how significant this was at the time. It wasn't until years later that Don happened to run into Rob at the beach and was able to tell him how much that act meant to him.

Although Don and I have been married for over twenty-three years, it is still hard for me to fully understand the pain Don lives with daily. I see suffering on his face on a particularly bad "nerve pain" day. His exaggerated limp tells me when his low back is aggravated. And sometimes I catch a glimpse of emotional pain when he's unable to lift a suitcase or help me move a piece of furniture. I remember the mixture of pain and joy I once saw on Don's face when we were over at our friends' swimming pool. Our friend Jerry picked up our daughter Heather and flung her into the deep end of the pool. I saw Don's joy at seeing her giggle and scream and his pain that his disability prevented him from playing with Heather in the same way. My heart has ached for my husband, who loves to be active but pays the price for physical activities that others take for granted.

DRAWING FROM YOUR HISTORY

This is part of Don's history, which is now part of our life together. As much as that history has prohibited certain activities, it has also enriched our lives. It has provided us both with a greater capacity for empathy.

Your histories are like individual cisterns. They hold gallons of information that can provide you and your mate with life-sustaining water. As you share from your cisterns of history with one another, the information forms a vast reservoir from which you may draw. Much like rainwater, which is filtered to remove contaminants from the atmosphere before it is drunk, the information shared between you may have to be filtered through the screen of God's love. Once it has been filtered, you can store it for future use. When seasons of drought hit your marriage, your reservoir becomes the source of a rich supply, irrigating your thirsty souls and enriching your life together.

Early in our marriage when I went to Don about the emotional pain from my past, God used Don's history of back pain as a reference point. He really didn't understand why my past abuse was eking its way into our lives. He wasn't sure he believed in counseling to aid in healing past hurts. He was a basketball coach with a coach's mentality: when a player gets hurt on the court, you pull him out of the game, tape him up, and get him back in the game. Initially, Don looked at me in much that way until God spotlighted his own pain. No one could see it, but he lived with it daily. He realized that I would support anything that might bring him relief, and he should do no less for me. He drew from the cistern of his own painful history and encouraged me to get the help I needed, even though it meant personal sacrifice for us both.

If I could, I would take away Don's pain — but I am also grateful for it. It was because of his pain that he could show me such compassion. You might be saying, "That's easy for her to say; she hasn't been the one suffering for thirty-eight years!" But we all carry injuries that limit us. The question is, what do we do with them?

Paul tells us what suffering is about:

Praise be to the God and Father of our Lord Jesus Christ, the Father of compassion and the God of all comfort, who comforts us in all our troubles, so that we can comfort those in any trouble with the comfort we ourselves have received from God. *(2 Corinthians 1:3-4, emphasis added)*

Paul says God gives us our troubles so that we might receive His comfort and, in turn, offer that comfort to others. This is called empathy. It is an endearing quality in any relationship and an enduring quality in a marriage.

EMPATHIC CONNECTION

What is empathic connection? Simply, it is the ability to feel another's feelings without being submerged by them and to respond to them with compassion. Don responded to my pain with compassion after empathetically connecting my pain to his own experience of pain.

Couples who create and maintain empathic connection experience a deeper, more intimate relationship than those who lack this capacity. I find that couples who work to develop this skill and practice it regularly find that their relationship is enriched as years go by. Marriages where this is not cultivated often become stale.

Betsy and Brian had been married seventeen years. Brian was the extrovert and communicator in the relationship. Betsy had struggled with depression for a few years by the time she came to see me. Her background included a father who was unavailable and a mother who had multiple marriages and showed little support for Betsy growing up. Betsy, now in her thirties, had everything she had dreamed of before she married. She had a lovely home with three daughters, she was a homemaker, and Brian had a stable job that provided well for the family. Brian was constantly on the go, involved in church activities and networking with men in the community. Betsy was a much more internal person who had difficulty establishing friendships with women and found it uncomfortable to reach out. Brian and Betsy loved each other, but their marriage was on shaky ground.

They found it difficult to relate to each other emotionally due to their differences in temperament. As a result, considerable distance developed between them and they had limited understanding and patience for one another. They were frustrated with each other because it seemed as though they were heading in different directions.

After Betsy was in counseling for a few months, we decided it was time to bring Brian into the process to help bridge some of the struggles they were experiencing as a couple. I spent a few weeks getting to know Brian and listening to how he saw their marriage. He was sincere and knew that Betsy was hurting, but he thought the solution was for her to be more assertive and reach out to the women at church who he knew wanted to be her friend.

I taught Brian and Betsy a Speaker/Listener technique. I had them use it while in session and practice it at home.[1] In session one evening, I asked Betsy to share with Brian how she was feeling. The following conversation ensued.

Betsy looked at Brian with tears in her eyes and said, "I feel alone in this marriage."

Brian, who had been taught to paraphrase what he heard, said in a matter-of-fact tone, "So, you feel alone in this marriage."

I stopped them both and asked Betsy to close her ears so I might talk to Brian. She did so, and in a quiet tone I said, "Brian, you paraphrased Betsy's words accurately, but I wonder if you understand what she is really saying. Has there ever been a time in your life when you've felt very alone? I want you to take a minute and think about that."

Brian paused, and then his eyes filled with tears. "When I was five years old, I went with my mother to a department store and got lost. I still remember how alone I felt. It was really scary and I didn't know what to do. It seemed to last forever."

I said, "Okay, that's good. What you were feeling *then* is what Betsy is feeling in your marriage. Take that experience and relate it back to Betsy in a way that she will know that you understand how she's feeling."

Betsy removed her fingers from her ears, and Brian looked into her eyes. He began gently, "Betsy, a few minutes ago you said to me that you feel alone in this marriage. I think I'm able to understand that a little better now. Honey, when I was five years old, I went with my mom to a big department store and got lost. I still remember how overwhelming it was. I was so scared and felt all alone. I hear you saying that is how you are feeling in our marriage. I'm so sorry; you must be feeling scared and overwhelmed."

Betsy immediately burst into tears and said, "That is the first time in seventeen years that I've felt as though you've heard me."

They hugged each other for a long time while I sat quietly. This was a sacred moment. Two hearts touched and healing had begun. This certainly was not the last time they were in counseling, nor was it the fateful leap across the chasm of distance that had taken years to create. But it was a significant step toward a new intimacy that would change their relationship. The journey was ahead, but the way had been paved.

Sharing your history can build intimacy and deepen your love and commitment. Unfortunately, some couples use it to tear each other down. Have you ever been to a dinner party where the host uses every occasion to blast a barb at his wife or comments to his guests about her incompetence? Or have you witnessed a wife who says, "Harry? Fix the plumbing? He can't fix breakfast in the morning!" Couples who use their mate's history against them only tear down the house in which they are living.

Instead of using each other's history for tearing each other down, why not use it as a means of building each other up? And how would that be done?

GROUND RULES

Let's look at some ground rules for sharing our histories. First, in order for sharing to take place, there must be a level of safety. This means that couples must agree not to use the material shared as a weapon in conflict or for public ridicule. Second, there must be mutual respect. Your experiences and responses may differ from your mate's. Third, an attitude of support is essential for vulnerable sharing. This means that you both approach your sharing and listening time with a genuine desire to uphold and comfort the other person. Finally, make sure you and your mate have set aside time for this activity. It can be hurtful to your sharing partner if interruptions or other matters distract you from giving him or her your full attention. This doesn't mean you'll never enter into this type of sharing spontaneously. Some of the sweetest times Don and I have shared have not been scheduled. But in the beginning, make it a practice to check in with each other to make sure you both can commit time to this and are on the same timetable.

This type of sharing may come easily for some and not so easily for others. I suggest you limit the time to about thirty minutes or less. Those who are "external processors" of information will find half an hour limiting because they are probably just getting warmed up. But those who are "internal processors" will find thirty minutes a huge amount of time to share. Most of us need repetition and practice when developing a new skill or improving an existing skill, so don't be afraid to schedule several times a month for this activity.

What guidelines should you use for the content of what you share? It is usually safe to begin talking with your mate about childhood experiences. You could share relatively safe things, such as how your family spent Christmas Day or the vacations you remember that were significant. If sharing your history is new for you as a couple, don't start off with the most traumatic experience of your life. Practice the skill of sharing and listening together on lighter topics until you have grown accustomed to this type of exchange.

Guidelines for the speaker include:

- Describe your experience (what happened, who was there)
- Describe how you felt during this experience (or how you feel now looking back)
- Describe how this experience affected you (how it shaped you)

Guidelines for the listener include:

- Listen from your heart (integrate emotions)
- Listen to understand your mate better (gain his or her frame of reference)
- Listen to respond in a reparative way (empathic connection)

One of Don's fondest memories growing up was living in Japan.

His father, who was in the navy, was stationed in Sasebo, Japan, from 1956-57. When we first married, Don often talked about that period of his life: playing in the old bunkers still standing from the war, running behind the truck that regularly sprayed DDT in the surrounding fields, and getting to know their Japanese maid named "Mama-san."

When he and his sisters traveled back to Japan recently, his sisters were amazed that Don could navigate around town with such precision. He led them to several places they'd been as children, and they stood outside the actual apartment on the naval base where they had lived forty-five years earlier. Don visited the bunkers where he had played, and his sister took a picture of him by a huge rock he climbed on as a boy. He shared the pictures of this memorable trip with his mother just three months before she died. Overall, those were happy times for him and his family.

There was another story, however, that Don shared about an experience with his father that hurt him.

INTIMATE SHARING

When I (Don) was eight, my father invited me to caddy for him in a golf game on the base. Since my father didn't initiate too many outings, I was excited about being with him and the other naval officers. I can still see that day in my mind. The golf course bordered the Pacific Ocean, and on that sunny summer day, the sun glistened off the water. Before teeing off, my father asked me to hold his watch while he played. Somewhere around the fifth hole, I picked up a few small rocks to skip along the water. I flung a stone across the water, and my father's watch slipped off my arm and went flying into the air. It fell on a boulder and smashed. My father was furious. He ran over to me screaming and kicked me in the seat of the pants while the other men watched. I was humiliated. The day I had so looked forward to ended in shame and rejection.

I told Jan this story a few years into our marriage with little emotion. Then one night, about ten years into our marriage, we were sharing with one another about how we both lacked a good father image because of our histories and how that loss had affected our spiritual lives. Jan asked me to tell the story of the golf course again. This time as I told it, I wept. I poured out the emotion I had held inside for decades. We hugged, prayed, and asked Father God to heal us and help us know His love at a deeper level.

There is something tremendously sacred about those moments in relationship with your mate. The curtain of the innermost chamber of his or her heart has been opened to you — you are invited into a sanctum where others have never been allowed. It is hallowed ground upon which you must tread lightly, but it is the bedrock of intimacy upon which your marriage is secured.

Ken Gire writes about this intimacy:

> In the Book of Proverbs, a book of universal wisdom, Solomon states that God's revelation goes beyond the universal to the personal. God, he tells us, "is intimate with the upright" (Proverbs 3:32). The word intimate means "private counsel." The Hebrew root means "to be tight, firm, pressed together," and one of its derivatives is the word for pillows or cushions, which are pressed together on a bed or couch. The derivative in Proverbs 3:32 means being pressed closely together for the purpose of confidential communication. The

word is used of lovers whose heads lie pressed next to each
other on pillows, where they reveal softly spoken intimacies
with each other. The word is also used of friends who share
their thoughts while sitting close together on a couch. . . .
Personal relationships like these are sustained by mutual rev-
elation. The more intimate the relationship, the more inti-
mate the revelation.[2]

I think that statement works both ways—the more intimate the revelation or disclosure, the more intimate the relationship becomes. God made us for relationship. First and foremost, He made us for a personal, intimate relationship with Himself. I love that God gave us so many relational pictures in the Scripture when he spoke of people. He called Abraham a "friend of God," Enoch "walked with God," David was a man "after [God's] own heart," and "The LORD would speak to Moses face to face as a man speaks to his friend" (James 2:23, KJV; 2 Chronicles 20:7; Genesis 5:22,24; 1 Samuel 3:14; Acts 13:22; Exodus 33:11).

In the New Testament, Jesus embodies God's desire to "dwell among us." He gave us His Spirit to be our constant companion. He speaks to His disciples and to us about intimacy in John 14 and 15:

On that day you will realize that I am in my Father, and you
are in me, and I am in you. Whoever has my commands and
obeys them, he is the one who loves me. He who loves me
will be loved by my Father, and I too will love him and show
myself to him. *(John 14:20-21, emphasis added)*

Jesus makes a distinction in chapter 15 about the nature of a relationship with a servant and that of a friend:

*Greater love has no one than this, that he lay down his life
for his friends. You are my friends if you do what I com-
mand. I no longer call you servants, because a servant does
not know his master's business. Instead, I have called you
friends, for everything that I learned from my Father I have
made known to you. (John 15:13-15)*

In other words, intimate relationship implies disclosure and
connection. God is a relational God, and since we are made in His
image, we are made for relationship — both with Him and others.

In a marriage, intimacy is visible. Think for a minute about
couples you know. Who in your circle of friends or family would
you say has an intimate relationship? What are characteristics of
those couples?

Intimacy goes beyond tolerance. It even goes beyond acceptance. Intimacy reflects enjoyment. One can usually tell by a couples' interaction whether or not they truly enjoy each
other — even amidst their differences. John Gottman, a well-
known researcher on marriage, states: "At the heart . . . is the simple truth that happy marriages are based on a deep friendship. By
this I mean a mutual respect for and enjoyment of each other's
company."[3]

HEARING FROM THE HEART

We've talked about sharing your history and how, in doing so, intimacy can be built. What part does listening play in the development of your relationship?

Think for a moment about any relationship in which one person
does all the talking and the other person does all the listening.
There will not be a great deal of intimacy. Intimacy is built

through mutual exchange — sometimes you are the speaker and your mate is the listener, and vice versa. Even in our relationship with God, we must allow for times of listening as well as times of speaking. Eddie Ensley says we often neglect a crucial part of relationship with God — listening. "In short, instead of praying, 'Speak Lord, your servant is listening,' we pray, 'Listen Lord, your servant is speaking.'"[4]

Listening is more than hearing with your ears. If sharing your history is to build intimacy, an open heart must welcome it. You need a heart that is willing to enter into the emotional realm of what is being shared.

Recently we had dinner with a group of people Don knew through coaching. Nine of us met together to celebrate the induction of a coach and basketball player into the California Community College Hall of Fame. The player was a young woman who played for a friend of Don's at a local community college. Jamie was there with her parents and was being honored the following day for her achievements on the court.

I was the only one at the table who was not acquainted with Jamie or her parents. Just as dessert was being served, Don asked Jamie if she was prepared for her talk the next morning. She replied that she was working on it. Then someone asked if she was going to share about her near-death experience. Everyone at the table except me knew what this question referred to. One of the other women at the table said, "I know about what happened, but I've never heard the entire story."

Jamie's mother told how Jamie contracted spinal meningitis when she was seventeen and how they almost lost her. For about twenty-five minutes her mother enraptured us by recounting the events. As I looked across the table at this young woman, full of life, and heard the impassioned account of this experience, I was moved. I was hearing with my ears, but it was my heart that was activated. I couldn't help feeling the fear of a mother faced with the possibility of losing her child. I could feel the confusion and dread of a dad who was called off the football field to the hospital. I pondered how my faith would stand if such circumstances unfolded with my own daughters. I didn't need to know this family well to empathize with them — all I needed to do was to let my heart engage.

Listening with your heart simply means that you let your heart engage. You allow yourself to feel the feelings that another person is or might be experiencing in a given situation. You integrate information with emotions. This skill is essential for building intimacy. You don't need to have the same or similar experiences to identify with someone. You need only the willingness to enter in emotionally, to walk in someone else's shoes.

Jesus often modeled this skill. The event that stands out in my mind is in John 11, when Jesus went to Lazarus' tomb:

> When Jesus saw [Mary] weeping, and the Jews who had
> come along with her also weeping, he was deeply moved in
> spirit and troubled. "Where have you laid him?" he asked.
> "Come and see, Lord," they replied. Jesus wept. (John
> 11:33-35, emphasis added)

I don't believe that Jesus was weeping over Lazarus' death, for He was about to raise him from the dead. Rather, I think Jesus was responding in compassion to the agony of those who had lost someone they loved. The words "moved" and "troubled" in Greek speak of "agitation or stirring."[5] I think of the word *churning*. Jesus did not rebuke the family for their feelings; rather, He entered in with tears and tenderness.

LISTENING TO LEARN

Along with hearing from our heart, we need to listen to understand our mate better. Al and Maria came into counseling for an ongoing issue in their marriage. It seemed that each time Al took a business trip, Maria came unglued. She asked Al to make sure he called the minute his plane landed, when he got to the hotel, and before he retired for the evening. If, by chance, he neglected to call, Maria phoned the hotel, left frantic messages, and asked the hotel personnel to page him over the intercom. Al had to travel at least once a month and could not stand that Maria was trying to control his every move. He resented her and would refuse to call her, insisting that her demands were outrageous.

After spending a few sessions together, I realized what was driving Maria's demands. When she was twelve, her parents left her and her brother with some friends from church while they attended a conference in a nearby city. The following day, news of her parents' fatal automobile accident was on the front page of their local paper. Although the church family rallied around Maria and her brother, life as she knew it was gone. No relatives lived locally, so Maria and her brother had to leave their home and everything that was familiar, on top of losing their parents. Although Al knew these facts, he didn't initially make the connection between his leaving town and the emotional trauma it evoked in Maria.

I taught Al and Maria about the value of sharing each other's history and helped them in the art of listening. By engaging emotionally as Maria shared the details of losing her parents, Al could better understand why she became so frightened each time he traveled. Maria did not immediately get over her fears, as she still had to grieve the loss of her parents. However, Al's willingness to understand and show compassion for Maria's history brought renewed comfort to their relationship. They worked together to modify Maria's demands, coming up with a plan that took into consideration Maria's fears and Al's need for realistic independence.

Listening in order to understand our mate better is part of working toward greater intimacy. When we listen with the intent to gain understanding and embrace our mate's point of reference, it takes the sting out of many a conflict.

Early in our marriage, when I was dealing with the history of my sexual abuse, it was difficult to engage in sexual intimacy with Don. At first, he had trouble understanding why those events had anything to do with our lovemaking. After educating himself about the impact of abuse and hearing my experience, he realized that as a child I had no choice about being abused. I was overpowered and required to submit to something that was hurtful and confusing at the hand of someone who was supposed to love and care for me. Through gaining this understanding, Don saw how important it was to approach our lovemaking gently and without coercion. He adopted a no-pressure policy and gave me the right of refusal. This self-sacrificing approach helped me trust Don and heal.

REPARATIVE RESPONSE

As time went on, our sexual relationship healed considerably. There were times, however, when I would have a setback. Sometimes it would be triggered by a flashback; at other times I was just feeling vulnerable. One night I'll never forget. We had experienced wonderful closeness and intimacy for several months. Yet this particular night as we were caressing and approaching lovemaking, I shut down and could not respond. I wasn't sure what had happened or why. Don pulled me in close and said, "Honey, it's okay. We don't have to make love tonight. I plan to spend the next fifty years with you, Lord willing. In light of fifty years, making love tonight doesn't matter."

I can't tell you what Don's response meant to me. It was what we call a reparative response. To listen and respond in a reparative way simply means that you respond to your mate in a way that repairs or brings comfort to hurts caused by his or her history. Such responses cannot be faked or calculated but come naturally from your intimate understanding and love for your mate.

Can reparative responses be learned? Absolutely. The prerequisites include the type of listening we've already talked about. You must be able to listen from the heart and integrate your emotions when your mate is sharing something from his or her history. You also must take time to try to understand your spouse better and the effect his or her history imposed. When you have done these two things, you are in position to respond in a reparative way.

To respond reparatively, you must give thoughtful consideration to how your mate has been shaped or injured by the experiences shared. For instance, Don's father was extremely impatient with him regarding household repairs. In exasperation, his father would grab a tool from Don's young hand and say, "Just give it to me! You can't do anything right." Unfortunately, early in our marriage I reinjured Don on many occasions by showing my own frustration over his inability to fix something around the house. I would say, "Just let me do it!" and Don would walk away in defeat. As Don shared these hurtful experiences with me, I finally realized how much he needed a healing response. I've tried since then to encourage him and find ways to praise him when he attempts something handy around the house. We've also learned as a couple how to take these things to God.

DIVINE REPARATIVE RESPONSE

One late night in bed we were sharing our hearts, and Don brought up this very subject. He talked about how hard it was for him to feel like a man in many ways because his father never took the time to teach him. I listened as he poured out the numerous times his father broke promises, disappointed him, or neglected to instruct him in manliness. We wept together, and then I suggested we pray. I prayed, "Lord, you know how Don's heart aches over these things. His father missed out on so much of what it means to be a dad. Lord, would you please be the Dad to Don that he didn't have? Would you show him what it means to be a man? Thank you, Lord for loving him as your son." We held each other for a long time and then drifted off to sleep.

The next morning our doorbell rang. At the door stood our neighbor, George. We had lived next door to George and his wife, Kay, for over six years, and to my recollection, this was the only Saturday morning George had ever come to our door.

George greeted me and then said, "Is Don here?"

I noticed that George had some kind of gadget in his hand. George said, "I noticed there are a couple of sprinklers in your front yard that aren't working properly. I came over to show Don how to fix them." I could hardly believe my ears. I hurried to find Don, who accompanied George to our front lawn. As soon as Don came in the door, I ran to his side. "Honey, what a faithful Father we have. He sent George as an answer to our prayer! He loves you so much that He would speak to George to teach you how to fix a sprinkler head." To this day, George has no idea how God used him to heal Don's broken heart.

God is bigger than our history. He is emotionally acquainted with it, He understands how it has affected us, and He desires to respond to it in a reparative way. He often uses people as the agents of His external repair work while His Spirit busily works to complete the internal work.

Maybe you are sensing your own need for repair. Do you realize that the same principles we outlined in this chapter concerning your mate also apply in relationship to God? In other words, if you want to build intimacy with God, you can apply these same guidelines! Decide to share your history with God in detail. Tell Him what happened, how you felt, and how it seems to have affected you. Realize that God is listening from an open heart of love. He understands you completely but wants to help you understand Him more. He wants to respond to you. Isaiah 61:1 describes Jesus' mission: God the Father "has sent me to bind up the brokenhearted." That word for "bind up" literally means to "wrap securely."

Envision being wrapped up securely in God's love. It reminds me of when my daughters were babies. I often wrapped them in what at that time was called a "snuggly." It was a sort of backpack that was worn by mothers across their chest. I would slip my daughter in, and she would rest her head against my breast. She was totally secure. Only her little feet and the top of her head were peeking out of the cocoon I strapped across my chest. I was "arms free" to do my chores or go to the market with my child safely affixed to my torso. She was comforted by the sound of my heartbeat and the warm encasement in which she had been placed. No one could get to her without coming through me. I think this is the picture God wants us to embrace. His love has a binding-up effect. Where we have been broken, torn, or wounded, He wraps His love securely around us to bring healing, warmth, and security. When we share our history with Him and seek His reparative response, He invites us into the secure wrappings of His love, and we are healed.

Take time to listen to Him. Listen from your heart. Listen to understand Him and yourself better. Listen for His reparative response to you. As you do, you will find deeper intimacy with Him. Intimacy with God and your mate is part of His design. It comes from sharing your history in an environment of safety. It requires integrating feelings and responding in reparative ways to your mate. When you share in this way, your history actually helps you grow. The healing balm of love replaces the ill effects of that history.

CHAPTER 10

WHOSE BAGGAGE IS WHOSE?

WE'VE TALKED ABOUT HOW TO USE YOUR SHARED HISTORIES to build intimacy in your relationship. When your house is framed with the strong timbers of love and safety, it can support cathedral ceilings and grand balconies without risk of collapse. Once a basic structural work is in place, you're ready to venture into cellars and attics that earlier may have felt too dangerous to explore. God wants to renovate all of it to give you back a home that is better than you dreamed. All He asks is for you to give Him access.

The metaphor of baggage can help you understand this deeper work. The deep work of restoration simply requires that you learn how to distinguish your baggage from your mate's.

YOURS, MINE, OR OURS?

Recently I (Don) and my sisters traveled to Japan together. It was a trip I'd dreamed about. We hadn't been back in forty-five years.

I've always been a light traveler, so off I went to Los Angeles International Airport with my carry-on and one small black roller bag checked through to Tokyo's Narita Airport. The flight was trouble-free, and we arrived at the bustling Narita airport the following afternoon. Even though I've traveled a lot and lived in

Japan for two years, it was striking to look around and see everything in Japanese. Nothing was in English. We navigated through the airport by following pictures of luggage to the baggage claim area. The Japanese are very efficient, and the bags were rounding the carousel when we arrived. I saw my bag, pulled it off, and placed it near me. Then I returned to the carousel to help my sisters retrieve their bags. We pulled our luggage to the customs area and were ushered through with no hassles.

The next challenge was to purchase tickets for the train that would take us to Tokyo Station. We maneuvered through the airport to the downward escalator leading to the subway. I felt good about how we had managed thus far. It had been a relatively easy transition; soon we would be on our way to our memories.

As we waited for the train that was due to arrive in fifteen minutes, my sister Diann said, "Don, that is not your bag."

"Sure it is," I said. "I checked it when I pulled it off."

"Look at the nametag — it's not yours."

I looked at the name and started sweating profusely. Panic set in. I went up the escalator and approached two policemen. They had no idea what I was saying. I grabbed the bag, retraced my steps to the customs area, and found no one there. On my way back, I found another police officer, who smiled but couldn't speak English. Back I went to the train station. Diann calmly suggested that we return upstairs to the United Airlines customer service counter. As we headed up yet again, my heart was pounding. *What am I going to do? Twelve days in Japan without my stuff?*

When my turn at the counter came, I started firing words at the United employee. Diann touched my arm and said, "Calm down. They know you're upset and they want to help you, but you need to lower your voice. Don, have you prayed?" I breathed a prayer. In a few moments, the agent instructed me to go to the customs area, and Diann returned to wait for the train. I wound around the hallways, backtracking my steps, and arrived to find my bag waiting for me. The customs officials checked my identification and thoroughly searched my bag before releasing me again. My heart kept pounding as I surged through the crowds to the underground subway where my sisters waited. I arrived with the bag mere moments before the train did.

Here's what I think happened. After I pulled my bag off the carousel, someone else must have placed a similar looking bag near mine. Then I helped my sisters with their bags. I didn't recheck the tag on my bag but simply wheeled away the one I thought was mine.

If you do much traveling by air, you know how easy it is to make a mistake like this. So many bags look alike! But the bottom line for travelers is, you're responsible for your own baggage. You're responsible for its contents. You're responsible to have it properly identifiable — and you're responsible to claim it when it arrives at your destination. The same is true for the "baggage" you carry into your marriage. The difficulty for many is properly identifying whose baggage is whose when it arrives at the door of your married life.

Remember, your baggage is anything you've carried into your marriage that plays itself out in an undesirable way. It can be the lack of a necessary skill or an unhealthy pattern in which you repeatedly get stuck. If you have trouble identifying *your* baggage, you might refer back to the warning signs and assessment tool in chapter 3 or think about what your mate's chief complaint is. Although our mates are not flawless in their perceptions, they offer us the opportunity to explore areas in which we may be blinded. Gary Thomas writes, "What marriage has done for me is to hold up a mirror to my sin. It forces me to face myself honestly and consider my character flaws, selfishness, and anti-Christian attitudes, encouraging me to be sanctified and cleansed and to grow in godliness."[1]

In Ephesians 4:15, Paul sets forth a principle crucial to the healthy development of the body of Christ. It is applicable to building a strong marriage: "Instead, speaking the truth in love, we will in all things grow up into him who is the Head, that is, Christ."

Sometimes it's necessary for you to speak the truth in love to your mate, and other times you need to listen to truth spoken. Don't miss that important phrase, "in love." In fact, a literal rendering of the phrase in Greek would be "truthing in love." It has the "idea of maintaining truth in love in both speech and life."[2] We have both had to speak the truth in love to each other many times over the last twenty-three years — but as we have, God has used that truth to help us grow.

SEASONED WITH GRACE

When our oldest daughter, Heather, was seventeen, it seemed like she and I (Jan) could not have a conversation without one of us snapping at the other or stomping out of the room. One warm summer night after another such episode, Don and I took a walk around our block. In frustration I said, "I can't understand it. We can't even talk to each other without it ending in a huge blowup. I can't figure out what is wrong!" Don stopped on the sidewalk, turned to me, and in his gentle tone asked, "Do you *really* want to know?"

One part of me wished I'd never posed the question, but I

knew whatever he was about to say had value, so I said, "Yes, I really want to know."

"Jan, almost every time you have a conversation with Heather, it starts out fine. Then, something changes. You get a condescending tone in your voice, and she reacts to it."

I'd love to say that I responded to my husband's wisdom maturely. I didn't. I said, "Fine! I'll never talk to her again."

By this time, we were halfway around the block. It took me the rest of the way home to say to Don, "I know you're right. But honey, I can't tell when I'm talking in that tone. Would you help me? When you hear me start to use that tone with her, would you signal me in some way from across the room? I need your help, because I'm not sure when I'm using that tone of voice."

Don put his arm around me and reassured me. He gave me a few pointers, and then we agreed on some signals he would use to tell me I was at it again. Over the next few months, signals flashed across the room like lights at a railroad crossing. Slowly my tone changed, and we weathered that stage of adolescence with only a few scrapes and a slightly wounded ego.

Several verses later in Ephesians 4:29, Paul says that our words should "build up" and "benefit" the hearer. In Greek, the word *benefit* literally means to "give grace or enablement to the hearer."[3] Don spoke the truth in love, and it enabled me to change a pattern that was hurtful to a relationship I valued. Without his input, I most likely would have remained blind to what was causing turmoil in my relationship with Heather. An added benefit was that my love and respect for Don grew as well. He loved me enough to share a difficult truth in order to bring about a greater good. That is the kind of love that helps us grow and become more Christlike.

BAG TAGS

What about you and your baggage? What comes to your mind when you think of the baggage you have carried into your marriage? Is it your control issues? Selfishness? Insecurities? Do you withdraw emotionally? Or have difficulty managing your anger? Do you struggle with sexual inhibitions or obsessions? Defensiveness? Do you give in to avoid conflict? Do you have trouble identifying and sharing your feelings?

One way that many travelers have adopted to help identify their baggage is to place some type of distinguishable tag, ribbon, or marker on each bag. When the baggage comes around the carousel at the airport, they can spot it readily.

When it comes to baggage in your marriage, is there an easy way to identify whose baggage is whose? What identifying markers or tags can you find to help you recognize your baggage from that of your mate's?

We've found three identifiers helpful in our marriage:

- Recurring themes
- Common triggers
- Reactive tendencies

RECURRING THEMES

Issues in marriage can be predictable. There are themes you can count on. Certain themes seem to surface within your relationship over and over again. Here are some common ones:

- Money
- Sex
- Communication

- Parenting

- Decision making

- In-laws

- Friends

Often, within these broad issues are *underlying themes* that stem from your history. For instance, if as a child your decisions were often criticized or questioned, you may have difficulty being definitive. This underlying theme may operate in more than one of the categories above. In money management, you might tend to be overly cautious and fearful about your future. In parenting, you might tend to second-guess yourself and feel guilty about the time-out you gave your six-year-old. In communicating with your mate, you may not feel your opinion is worth sharing.

Recurring themes tend to crop up repeatedly and most often have historical roots. These roots may be from our growing-up years or from adult experiences prior to marriage. For example, Stan was previously married and divorced. He'd been single for five years before he met and married Linda. During the first year of their marriage, their sexual relationship was good, but slowly over the next seven years it became almost nonexistent. Linda was confused and hurt. It seemed like Stan had no interest or motivation. After seeking counseling, Stan and Linda learned that their problems had historical roots. Stan had been a victim of sexual abuse by an aunt who baby-sat him as a child. To complicate matters further, Stan's first wife used to criticize Stan's sexual performance. Even though Linda was not critical in their first year of marriage, as Stan's lack of desire increased, she voiced her concerns and in Stan's mind became more and more like the ex-wife whom he could not please. It took some considerable work to help Stan face his grief over the abuse he received as a child and the hurt that he'd felt in his first marriage, but Linda remained committed to loving and understanding Stan. Her commitment helped them both develop trust and intimacy. They were able to talk together about their feelings about sex and decide what was beneficial and nurturing to them both. Stan understood that Linda's needs had less to do with his sexual performance and more to do with wanting closeness with him. As they worked through these issues as a couple, their relationship deepened and broadened, and they were able to restore a healthy sexual relationship.

In addition to topical issues that repeat themselves, recurring themes may include *internalized messages* that are played out in your relationship. Some researchers believe that we marry in our mate the parent *with whom we had the greatest unresolved conflict*. We do this in an attempt to resolve what was never resolved in our families growing up. When I first heard this, I wondered whether it was valid. It wasn't until a few years into our marriage that I recognized how Don and I were struggling to correct previous messages that had been ingrained into the fabric of our souls.

Don married in me his critical, perfectionist father, whom he could never seem to please. I married in Don my passive, resigning mother, who did everything to avoid conflict and did not protect me as a child.

Both of us have seen these two recurring themes throughout our marriage. Don often feels his "efforts are never good enough," that he's "messed up again," and that he's "foolish for not taking care of business." All of these are messages that he received from his father growing up. I often feel "uncared for," that "my needs don't matter," and that I've been "abandoned and unprotected." All of these messages characterized my relationship with my mother.

Internalized messages may or may not be spoken directly to us, but they are lived out in behaviors and attitudes that are transmitted through our experience. As we mentioned earlier, all of us need to reconcile ourselves in these areas through forgiveness, but it sometimes takes time to unload the baggage we've carried for years. No matter what the current topic is, Don and I know that when our favorite themes come up, we are individually responsible for our side of the issue, for the messages echoing from our past. Identifying these themes is a way of tying a red tag to a bag so that when it appears on the baggage carousel, we know who should claim it.

What does that mean in practical terms? An illustration may help. Last Saturday morning, we had an appointment to take my car in to be serviced. I asked Don on Friday if he would call to see how long the service would take because I had an appointment at 1:30 P.M. and would need my car. He phoned and was told it would be done by 11:00 A.M. On Saturday morning he drove my car to the dealership, and I came a few minutes later to pick him up. On our way home, he said that they would not have the car done until after 2:00 P.M. I became upset. "What do you mean? They said yesterday it would be done by eleven o'clock! Did you tell them that was unacceptable?"

Don said, "No. I said it was fine. I'll just walk down to get the car, and you can take my car."

You can probably see the issues emerging in this scenario. Don felt I was saying he didn't do it right. I felt that my needs were unimportant to him and he wouldn't stand up to take care of me. We are often in the middle of the barrage of feelings before we get a handle on what is going on.

When we arrived home, we both sat down (separately) to pray. We asked the Lord to help us see through this situation and to help us resolve this minor infraction so it did not lead to an all-out war. Fortunately, we came together later and shared how we each were feeling. We recognized how our old internalized messages from our backgrounds were being activated. We listened to each other, confessed, and prayed together, asking God to help heal those old hurts so that we didn't continue to let them flare up in our relationship. We recommitted to being sensitive to and caring for each other as we interact, knowing that these "themes" are deep wounds into which neither of us wants to inflict more injury. We know that left to ourselves, we cannot change. But with humility and dependence upon God, we can allow His Spirit to transform us from the inside out.

Paul reminds us that we are inadequate in ourselves:

> Not that we are competent in ourselves to claim anything for ourselves, but our competence comes from God. . . . But we have this treasure in jars of clay to show that this all-surpassing power is from God and not from us.
> (2 Corinthians 3:5; 4:7)

Stop right now and think for a moment about any recurring themes that surface between you and your mate. How are these themes played out between you? If these themes stem from past relationships or a previous marriage, have you taken the necessary steps toward forgiveness and repair? Is there any indication that you are trying to resolve with your mate what was not resolved in your family? What are some of the internalized messages that you have carried into this relationship?

Take some time to pray over these questions. Ask the Lord to reveal where you have been wounded in the past and agree with Him about your need for His deep healing in your heart. If you can, share with your mate what you have discovered about yourself and pray together for restoration.

COMMON TRIGGERS

There was a popular television show in the 1970s entitled *All in the Family*, starring Carroll O'Connor and Jean Stapleton. O'Connor played Archie Bunker, a bigoted, self-proclaimed all-around expert. He dominated his wife, Edith, a sensitive but naïve, doting wife who catered to Archie's every need. Archie and his son-in-law, Mike, epitomized the conflict between the ultra-conservative bigot and the liberal youth of that decade. From week to week, the programs highlighted the arguments between Archie and anyone with whom he disagreed, which was most everyone. Viewers watched loyally as Archie spewed out bigotry and racism, some of which they recognized in themselves. I remember that my parents loved the show. I thought Archie was disgusting. We sat in our living room, mirroring the relationships portrayed on the screen. What was particularly interesting was the way viewers anticipated Archie or Mike's response to a given subject. Viewers could predict which comments would evoke an avalanche response by either Archie or Mike. You might say viewers became acquainted with the "triggers" that would set off either character.

Most of us have such triggers in relationships. These are the comments, attitudes, or behaviors that evoke from us an automatic response. These common triggers may indicate unresolved baggage.

One of my triggers is related to Archie and Edith. It bugged me to watch Archie sit in his lounge chair while Edith waited on him hand and foot. This was all too familiar in my home growing up. Today, if we are sitting at the dinner table and Don asks, "Is there any ketchup for the French fries?" he can bet I will retort, "Yes. It's in the refrigerator." He knows what that means: *you may get up and get it yourself, or if absolutely necessary, you may kindly ask me to get it for you.* Don agrees that I lovingly serve him—but when he has an unspoken expectation that I *should* serve him, my servant attitude goes out the window.

Triggers don't always spark anger. They may ignite depression, fear, anxiety, or hopelessness.

Debbie grew up in a home where her father was obsessed with her body. When she started to develop, he made inappropriate comments at the dinner table about her "blossoming." Her mother, on the other hand, would make comments to Debbie about "men and their sick need for sex." It is no wonder that when Debbie married, she had all kinds of baggage to work through regarding her attitudes about sex. Whenever her husband complimented her about anything, it triggered the notion that he was after "one thing," and she would distance herself to avoid intimacy.

What about you? What are some of your triggers? What flares your anger or sends you down the track of despair? How can you ask your mate for help or set boundaries for yourself to manage your reactions? Are there events that typically set you off? If so, do your responses match what the incident warrants, or are they exaggerated?

REACTIVE TENDENCIES

When was the last time you overreacted to a situation? What were the circumstances? What were you feeling inside? How did you feel when it was all over? Embarrassed? Ashamed? Justified? Guilty?

Most of us overreact sometimes. But what you may not know is the root issue from your background that is budding for recognition. In counseling over the years, I've discovered that our intense reactions to situations often have historical roots. In other words, when our reactions are extreme or above the norm, we should look to our history for understanding.

Reactive tendencies can be compared to the temperature gauge in your car. For the most part, your gauge stays at an even level. However, if it rises dramatically, you'd better check out the cause. Many things can make the temperature rise. The cause can be as simple as traveling uphill in warm weather, or it may be a more serious problem under the hood, like a radiator or alternator needing repair. In your life, the cause can be as simple as a rough day at work that has put you over the edge. Or it may be internal baggage that was hoisted to the surface by a familiar tone of voice or a disappointing review by your boss. Emotional reactivity can take the form of tears, anger, frustration, grief, or sadness. The current stimulus is only the activator of something residing beneath the surface of your emotions.

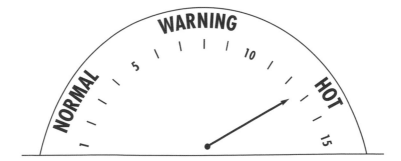

Normal Range   = 1–4   Emotional response appropriate to stimulus
Warning   = 5–9   Historical issues likely influencing response
Reactive Range = 10–15 Highly likely that emotional response is tied to
                         unresolved emotional baggage

Any given situation elicits a response. If the normal response to such a situation registers "2" on a scale of "1-15" in emotional intensity, and your response registers "12," it's worth exploring why your response was so intense.

Discovering whose baggage is whose is not always easy. It requires the ability to step back from the current situation and evaluate what is going on internally. If you and your mate find yourselves in a state of high drama, chances are that both of your histories are acting up.

Every few weeks, Michelle and Chuck entered what they called "cold war." It usually looked like this: Michelle would complain that Chuck had neglected to take out the trash. Chuck would then dutifully take out the trash but resent Michelle for always pointing out his shortcomings. Chuck would not speak to Michelle for hours. Michelle would notice that Chuck was distant and would wonder what was wrong. Neither would speak to each other about their perceptions or feelings.

Day one typically ended with a goodnight kiss on the cheek and icicles in the air. On day two, Michelle felt hurt and mad over Chuck's distance from her. Her anger spewed out in snippy comments that Chuck answered defensively. Both of them would isolate, justify their anger, and refuse to go to each other in humility. Sometimes this pattern would go on for weeks at a time — both of them were miserable, but neither knew what to do.

In counseling, I helped Michelle and Chuck understand the historical roots of their reactions. Chuck had an overcontrolling mother who was quick to point out his deficiencies. Every time Michelle reminded Chuck of something he'd forgotten to do, Chuck's unresolved anger would rise and he'd withdraw in the same way he did as a boy. Michelle's father deserted her and her family when she was six years old. Her father called occasionally but never made good on his promises. All Michelle's abandonment issues with her father flooded in when Chuck forgot a simple task and withdrew from the relationship.

After I encouraged Michelle and Chuck to share their feelings and taught them about empathic connection, we talked about a formula that helped them diminish the cold wars:

- Step 1: Recognize
- Step 2: Communicate
- Step 3: Determine the source

First, each person was to be responsible for recognizing emotional distancing patterns. It didn't matter who was the instigator; if one person was feeling distant, he or she was to own that feeling and communicate it to the other.

Second, the communication was to consist of "I" statements rather than "you" statements. *Do* say, "I'm not sure why this is happening, but I'm feeling distant from you right now." *Don't* say, "Ever since you got back from (shopping, golfing, or whatever), you have been in your own world. You have withdrawn from me again."

Third, determine the source and share it with your mate. If you are the one feeling distant, try to discover where this feeling originated and talk about the source with your mate using the speaker/listener skills from chapter 9. Sometimes the distance may have nothing to do with your mate. It may be related to work or just built-up frustration from your day. *Do* let your mate in on the source if you know it: "Honey, I'm feeling distant right now from everyone. An incident with a person at work has really upset me. I need some time to work this out."

Following these simple guidelines can reduce the reactivity and move you toward each other rather than away from one another.

Sometimes, just as in the case with your car, it may be helpful to explore emotional reactivity with a professional who can help you sort it out and discover how to use your history for growth in godliness.

You've learned to identify your baggage by looking for recurring themes, common triggers, and reactive tendencies. Don't be discouraged when you find these in your relationship. They indicate potential, not failure. If you feel overwhelmed by what look like suitcases full of themes, triggers, and overreactions, let yourself take time to unpack them all. And before you start dumping the contents of all this luggage onto your living room floor, prepare yourself and your mate by practicing the speaker / listener skills of chapter 9. Develop closeness as you unpack some of the lighter moments of your histories. Experiment with empathic connection. Choose a relatively simple issue and play with the *face-trace-erase-replace* process. Tackle the heavy stuff only when you're ready and at a pace you and your mate can handle.

And don't be embarrassed to seek help. There's probably someone in your life who would love to befriend you in this process. The Holy Spirit can also work through professional counselors and pastors.

Every day you have an opportunity to create a new history. And every day God will provide you with the grace and mercy to do so. If you question whether all this work is worth the effort, Don and I can say that while we'd probably still be together even if we hadn't done this work, our marriage would be a mere shell. We'd have missed the opportunity to live with a friend, an ally, a lover. More than that, we'd have missed the chance to give our daughters a model of what God longs for them to have in a marriage.

ACTION STEP: THIRTY DAYS OF PRAYER

If you're experiencing difficulties that are beyond your ability to resolve, we encourage you to do one thing before you do anything else. Commit to thirty days of daily prayer with your mate. If he or she is not open to praying with you, do it on your own. Ask God to show you the next step in the process of revitalizing your marriage. It may be the step of seeking professional counseling, it may be writing a letter of confession to your mate, it may be joining a support group, or it may be reading through some of the suggested material at the end of this book. In whatever direction God is leading you, determine to stay at it with God's help.

CHAPTER 11

HISTORY TO LAST
A LIFETIME

HAVE YOU EVER STOPPED AT THE END OF A DAY AND reflected on the history you made that day? I'm not talking about the kind that merits notation in the *Guinness Book of World Records*. I'm talking about the history you and I make every day, living our lives in relationship to others, especially our mates.

The truth is, like it or not, we make history every day. We've focused up to this point on the history that you have brought with you into your marriage. We've talked about what makes it up, the baggage that has resulted, how to reconcile it through forgiveness, and how you can use your history to help each other grow. You've learned how important it is to claim your baggage in order to unload the burden of it from your marriage so you can travel lighter to the glory of God.

We want to encourage you to start a new history through the process we've described in this book. You can't change your past history, but God can transform it and help you create a new history. That new history doesn't annihilate your previous history; it is birthed from it.

BIRTHING A NEW HISTORY

One of my favorite stories about Jesus is recorded in John 4. It is Jesus' encounter with the woman of Samaria. Most commentators agree that this encounter was highly irregular. In fact, although the shortest route from Galilee to Jerusalem was through Samaria, "the Pharisees avoided this customary route, and took a longer, round-about one through Peraea . . . to avoid contact with the Samaritans with whom, as Jews, they had no dealings."[1]

Jesus went this way intentionally. Why? He went to talk to a woman who had quite a history. In John 4:5, we read that Jesus came to a town in Samaria by the name of Sychar. It was around noon, in the heat of the day, when Jesus stopped to rest beside a well. As He was sitting there, a Samaritan woman came to draw water, and Jesus asked her to give Him something to drink. This was unusual. First, "the normal prejudices of the day prohibited public conversation between men and women, between Jews and Samaritans, and especially between strangers. A Jewish Rabbi would rather go thirsty than violate these proprieties."[2] Second, Jesus had nothing with which to draw water, so He would have to drink from her vessel. Drinking from the vessel of a nonJew would make Him ceremonially unclean.[3] Understandably, the woman was surprised by his request and asked, "You are a Jew and I am a Samaritan woman. How can you ask me for a drink?" (John 4:9).

Jesus went on to tell her that if she knew who He was, she would have asked Him for a drink, and He would give her "living water" (4:10). She asked about this living water, and He told her that the water He gave was like a "spring of water welling up to eternal life" (4:14). She asked Him to give her that water.

He told her to call her husband and then come back. She replied that she had no husband.

Then Jesus said something that would change her life forever. It wasn't a theological treatise or a doctrinal revelation. He simply, straightforwardly recounted her history. He said, "You are right when you say you have no husband. The fact is, you have had five husbands, and the man you now have is not your husband. What you have just said is quite true" (John 4:17-18).

In the ensuing conversation, Jesus told her that He was the promised Messiah. His disciples returned and were surprised to see Him talking with the woman. She left her water jar and hurried back to town to tell the people about her encounter. She invited them to, "Come, see a man who told me everything I ever did" (John 4:29).

I don't know about you, but I find this unusual. Imagine meeting a stranger at the car wash who asks you out of the blue to give him a lift somewhere. He goes on to say that if you knew who he was, you'd be asking *him* to give you a brand new luxury car that never needed any maintenance. Like the woman at the well, you'd say, "Bring it on. I could use a car like that." What if the man looked at you and then proceeded to tell you everything you'd ever done in your life? Every lie reported on your income taxes, every shameful thought, every bad decision—he laid it all out in front of you. Would you feel compelled to run to the center of your town shouting, "Come, see a man who told me everything I ever did"?

What caused her to go back with *that* message? Why didn't she say, "I just met a man who really understands the true essence of what it means to worship God—come and meet him"? Wouldn't that have gotten the point across without highlighting her humiliation?

Scripture doesn't tell us exactly why hearing her life history made such an impression, but I can't help but ponder some possibilities.

This was a woman of ill repute. Probably most in Sychar knew her or at least about her. Some scholars think she went to the well at midday to avoid the usual encounters with the other women who went earlier in the day to draw water. She had a history that followed her everywhere she went. In one sense, she couldn't get away from it. In another sense, she couldn't face it. So when she encountered Someone infinitely bigger than her history and the baggage she carried as a result, the experience captured her heart.

Jesus stepped in unexpectedly and offered her life. He offered her a new start — even though He knew everything about her. This was too good to be true. Even with a history like hers, she could start fresh. And it happened — in a moment. He loved her enough to help her face her past, to look at it squarely for what it was, and then to offer her life in spite of it. He was birthing in her a new history. That was the joy behind her proclamation to the townspeople: "Come, see a man who loves me right where I am. Come, see a man who looks beyond all that I have been and offers me hope for a future. Come, see a man who can transform a woman like me. Come, see a man . . . "

A FRESH START

This same offer is held out for you today as an individual and as a couple. It doesn't matter what your past has been. God wants to offer you a fresh start. That fresh start means that you must face your history squarely, as we've tried to help you do in this book. It involves claiming your baggage. It requires coming to grips with losses and patterns that have developed over time. It necessitates a priority and commitment to your marriage that is unparalleled in all other relationships except your relationship with God. It calls for reconciliation through forgiveness in all relationships — past, present, and future. It demands personal ownership and confession, as well as growth through suffering. It promises deeper intimacy and ushers you into a depth of oneness that God desires you to have with Him and your mate. It provides understanding, help, and encouragement in your growth in godliness. It promotes longevity and fulfillment unsurpassed by anything else this side of eternity. And it is available to you today.

It is not instantaneous, but it is sure. It is not easy, but it is secure. It is not effortless, but it does endure.

Don't think for a minute that the woman at the well didn't have some practical issues that she had to deal with after her encounter with Jesus. She had to face the man she was living with and make some hard decisions. She had to learn a new way of living. She had to come face to face with her pattern of looking to men for her security. She probably spent time reflecting on how and why that pattern had developed. She may have traced it back to something in her own background. She most likely came to the place of repentance and realized she needed to be reconciled to God and others through forgiveness. She knew that the life she had lived up to this point was not the life God had for her future. She had to start fresh — a new history that encompassed facing, tracing, erasing, and replacing what she had known.

This, however, was not the end of her story. In fact, we read in John 4:39-42 the amazing results of what transpired. "Many of the Samaritans from that town believed in him because of the woman's testimony." The people urged Jesus to stay longer with them, and many more came to believe. Finally, the townspeople said to the woman, "We no longer believe just because of what you said; now we have heard for ourselves, and we know that this man really is the Savior of the world."

Can you believe what took place from a simple request for a drink of water? In many ways, Don and I were like the woman of Samaria. We were going through the motions of our married life when God stepped in to offer us new life. He had us face our histories honestly, and with His help we went through the process of tracing, erasing, and replacing our history to establish a new history in Him. Gary Thomas writes, "Every wedding gives birth to a new history, a new beginning. The spiritual meaning of marriage is found in maintaining that history together."[4]

Like the woman at the well, we appeal to you, inviting you to "Come, see a man who was able to transform us in spite of our histories." In fact, He used our histories in the process of that transformation, and He can do that for you as well. We love nothing more than to hear from others who believe because they've experienced it for themselves, just like the people of Sychar.

A TESTIMONY OF TRANSFORMATION

Ed and Carrie are one of those couples. Both Ed and Carrie had come from alcoholic families, both had sexual abuse in their backgrounds, and both had been previously married. They were brand-new Christians when they married and had to deal with the issues of a blended family. Carrie had three children — ages eight, six, and five — from her previous marriage. Ed had none. They tried their best to come together as a family, but the children's weekend visitations with Carrie's ex-husband always seemed to bring turmoil back into their home.

They made some decisions early that helped. They decided not to have alcohol in their home while raising their children, understanding the impact alcoholism had on both their histories. They committed to each other to work together as a team since that was missing in their homes growing up. They committed to making their relationship a priority by instituting a date night, standing united with the kids, being honest with each other, agreeing not to put each other down in front of others, and not keeping secrets from one another.

They had managed to navigate through twenty years of marriage before I met them. They were struggling with anger toward each other and difficulty in their sexual relationship. It seemed like they continually reached an impasse when discussing finances, and although they loved each other, they were stuck and frustrated.

Initially, Ed and Carrie spent time taking inventory. They looked at the areas in their relationship that were valuable and then assessed where the repair work was needed. Both of them agreed that communication was a major issue, so we worked on building solid, healthy communication skills, which they practiced on a regular basis.

As they learned new methods of speaking and listening to each other, we used their history as the content of that dialogue. They shared with each other about their backgrounds and the impact those backgrounds had on them as children and later as adults. They learned how to face and trace their histories. In the process, Ed and Carrie discovered more about the origins of their marital struggles. During this phase, we did not emphasize problem solving as much as developing communication skills and empathy. Watching them interact and understand for the first time how painful some of the events in their histories had been was a profound experience. God was using the very wounds of their history to create a new history—a history of understanding, compassion, accountability, and growth.

Over the next three years, Ed and Carrie were diligent to reach for all that God desired for their marriage. It took perseverance as they worked through their history of hurt with each other, their families, their previous mates, and their now grown children. It took perseverance as they battled to overcome stubbornness and let go of the anger that had choked out the joy from their relationship. It took prayer and patience as they learned to let go of former patterns and implement new ways to solve their differences. And it took time.

God's transformation has yielded a harvest. Ed said recently, "What I've got now is gold—and it gets better daily." Carrie said, "It's not that it's perfect, but it's so wonderful to share my life with someone whom I totally trust. I can be myself and be loved." We all agreed, "Two are better than one, because they have a good return for their work" (Ecclesiastes 4:9).

Ed and Carrie don't have a history devoid of struggles. They do have a history to last them a lifetime—a history of redemption. Bill and Lynn Hybels wrote,

> In the covenant of marriage, God asks two self-willed sinners to come together and become one flesh—not in body only, but in spirit, in attitude, in communication, in love. Think about the implications. Imagine two self-willed sinners trying to submit to one another as God calls them to do. That will take a decade. Or imagine two self-willed sinners trying to serve one another joyfully. Another decade. Imagine two self-willed sinners trying to show honor to one another. Yet another decade. Or to encourage one another. Or to

edify one another. It is a lifetime challenge—perhaps the single greatest challenge there is.[5]

HISTORY FOR LIFE

You may feel totally inadequate to meet that challenge. If you do, you're not alone. You may be discouraged, and the enemy may be trying to get you to give up on your marriage. He may say it's too late, there's too much work to be done, and it's hopeless. Don't listen. Devote yourself to God, lean into Him, and rest in His unchanging grace at work in your life. Commit yourselves to going through the process we've described—it's worth it. God wants to help you rebuild and restore.

When I think back to the flood in our home nine years ago, it's hard to remember the emotional upheaval that accompanied that interruption. I look around my house now and realize that within these walls, Don and I have finished raising our two daughters, laughed at home movies, experienced the angst of the teen years, and most recently, endured the anguish of losing a mother. There are still repairs and maintenance projects that require more than we bargained for. The house needs painting, the air conditioner needs repair, and the towel rack is broken. But we are at home.

Likewise, we're at home in our marriage because of God's grace. We came into our marriage with histories that had the potential to flood our life with pain and misery. Instead, God has redeemed that history and used it to create a new history—a history to last a lifetime. He wants to do this in your marriage, too. Let Him have your history, your marriage, and your heart— He is in the restoration business, and He is able to redeem!

Put your hope in the LORD,
for with the Lord is unfailing love
and with him is full redemption.
(Psalm 130:7, emphasis added)

RECOMMENDED READING

MARRIAGE

Allender, Dan, and Tremper Longman. *Intimate Allies*. Wheaton,
    IL: Tyndale House, 1999.
Cloud, Dr. Henry, and Dr. John Townsend. *Boundaries in Marriage*.
    Grand Rapids, MI: Zondervan, 1999.
Parrott, Dr. Les, and Dr. Leslie Parrott, *When Bad Things Happen
    to Good Marriages*. Grand Rapids, MI: Zondervan, 2001.
Smalley, Gary. *Making Love Last Forever*. Dallas, TX: Word
    Publishing, 1997.
Thomas, Gary. *Sacred Marriage: What If God Designed Marriage to
    Make Us Holy More Than to Make Us Happy?* Grand Rapids,
    MI: Zondervan, 2002.

SEX

Dillow, Linda, and Lorraine Pintus. *Intimate Issues: Conversations
    Woman to Woman*. Colorado Springs, CO: Waterbrook, 1999.
Penner, Dr. Clifford, and Joyce Penner. *Men and Sex*. Nashville,
    TN: Thomas Nelson, 1997.

COMMUNICATION / CONFLICT RESOLUTION

Stanley, Scott, Daniel Trathen, Savanna McCain, and Milt
    Bryan. *A Lasting Promise: A Christian Guide to Fighting for Your
    Marriage*. Indianapolis, IN: Jossey-Bass, 1998.

ABUSE/DYSFUNCTIONAL FAMILY ISSUES

Allender, Dan. *The Wounded Heart.* Colorado Springs, CO: NavPress, 1990.

Frank, Jan. *Door of Hope: Recognizing and Resolving the Pains of Your Past.* Nashville, TN: Thomas Nelson, 1995.

Humbert, Cynthia Spell. *Deceived by Shame, Desired by God.* Colorado Springs, CO: NavPress, 2001.

Langberg, Diane M. *On the Threshold of Hope.* Wheaton, IL: Tyndale House, 1999.

Sell, Charles. *Helping Troubled Families: A Guide for Pastors, Counselors, and Supporters.* Grand Rapids, MI: Baker Books, 2002.

Wilson, Sandra. *Hurt People Hurt People.* Grand Rapids, MI: Discovery House, 2001.

Wilson, Sandra. *Released from Shame* (revised edition). Downer's Grove, IL: InterVarsity, 2002.

PERSONAL GROWTH

Cloud, Dr. Henry. *Changes That Heal: How to Understand the Past to Ensure a Healthier Future.* Grand Rapids, MI: Zondervan, 1992.

Cloud, Dr. Henry, and Dr. John Townsend. *Boundaries.* Grand Rapids, MI: Zondervan, 1992.

Cloud, Dr. Henry, and Dr. John Townsend. *How People Grow: What the Bible Reveals About Personal Growth.* Grand Rapids, MI: Zondervan, 2001.

Cloud, Dr. Henry, and Dr. John Townsend. *Safe People.* Grand Rapids, MI: Zondervan, 1996.

FORGIVENESS

Lynch, Dr. Chuck. *I Should Forgive, But . . .* Dallas, TX: Word
   Publishing, 1998.

Smedes, Lewis. *Forgive and Forget.* New York: Pocket Books, 1986.

NOTES

CHAPTER 1
1. Dr. Henry Cloud and Dr. John Townsend, *How People Grow: What the Bible Reveals About Personal Growth* (Grand Rapids, Mich.: Zondervan, 2001), p. 140.
2. Marian McFadden, *Feasting on the Word Studies: A Look at the Apostle Paul*, unpublished Bible study, 1998.
3. Max Lucado, *He Chose the Nails: What God Did to Win Your Heart* (Nashville, Tenn.: Word, 2000), pp. 65-66.

CHAPTER 2
1. Maggie Scarf, *Intimate Partners: Patterns in Love and Marriage* (New York: Random House, 1987), pp. 40-41.

CHAPTER 3
1. Maggie Scarf, *Intimate Partners: Patterns in Love and Marriage* (New York: Random House, 1987), pp. 40-41.
2. Claudia Black, *"It Will Never Happen to Me!": Children of Alcoholics As Youngsters–Adolescents–Adults* (New York: Ballantine, 1981), pp. 24-38.
3. Jan Frank, *Door of Hope: Recognizing and Resolving the Pains of Your Past* (Nashville, Tenn.: Thomas Nelson, 1995).
4. Charles Sell, *Unfinished Business: Helping Adult Children Resolve Their Past* (Portland, Oreg.: Multnomah, 1989), pp. 41-42.

CHAPTER 4
1. Dale Burke, *Different by Design: God's Master Plan for Harmony Between Men and Women in Marriage* (Chicago, Ill.: Moody Press, 2000), p. 177.
2. Ron and Betty Wiseman, *Enjoying Marriage* (Costa Mesa, Calif.: self-published, 1989), p. 88. www.enjoyingmarriage.org.

3. Wiseman, p. 88.
4. Maggie Scarf, *Intimate Partners: Patterns in Love and Marriage* (New York: Random House, 1987), p. 52.

CHAPTER 5

1. Gary Thomas, *Sacred Marriage: What If God Designed Marriage to Make Us Holy More Than to Make Us Happy?* (Grand Rapids, Mich.: Zondervan, 2000), p. 22.
2. Thomas, p. 26.
3. Thomas, p.133.

CHAPTER 6

1. Charles Sell, *Unfinished Business: Helping Adult Children Resolve Their Past* (Portland, Oreg.: Multnomah, 1989), p. 19.
2. Merriam-Webster, Incorporated, *Merriam Webster's Collegiate Dictionary*, 10th edition (Springfield, Mass.: Merriam Webster, 1994), p. 991.
3. Gary Thomas, *Sacred Marriage: What If God Designed Marriage to Make Us Holy More Than to Make Us Happy?* (Grand Rapids, Mich.: Zondervan, 2000), p. 186.
4. Howard Markman, Scott Stanley, and Susan Blumberg, *Fighting for Your Marriage: Positive Steps for Preventing Divorce and Preserving a Lasting Love* (San Francisco, Calif.: Jossey-Bass, 2001), pp. 110-114.
5. Scott Stanley, Daniel Trathen, Savanna McCain, and Milt Bryan, *A Lasting Promise: A Christian Guide to Fighting for Your Marriage* (San Francisco, Calif.: Jossey-Bass Publishers, 1998), pp. 76-82.

CHAPTER 7

1. W. E. Vine, *Vine's Expository Dictionary of New Testament Words* (MacLean, Va.: MacDonald, 1993), p. 942.
2. Chuck Smith, *Why Grace Changes Everything* (Eugene, Oreg.: Harvest House, 1994), p. 41.
3. David Seamands, *Healing of Memories* (Wheaton, Ill.: Victor, 1985), p. 95-96.
4. Vine, p. 637.
5. Dr. Henry Cloud and Dr. John Townsend, *How People Grow: What the Bible Reveals About Personal Growth* (Grand Rapids, Mich.: Zondervan, 2001), p. 128.
6. Jan Frank, *Door of Hope: Recognizing and Resolving the Pains of Your Past* (Nashville, Tenn.: Thomas Nelson, 1995), p. 118.

7. Gary Thomas, *Sacred Marriage: What If God Designed Marriage to Make Us Holy More Than to Make Us Happy?* (Grand Rapids, Mich.: Zondervan, 2000), p. 170.

CHAPTER 8

1. Dr. Henry Cloud and Dr. John Townsend, *Boundaries in Marriage* (Grand Rapids, Mich.: Zondervan, 1999), p. 64.
2. Dr. Clifford Notarius and Dr. Howard Markman, *We Can Work It Out* (New York: Penguin Putnam, 1993), p. 20.
3. Dr. Henry Cloud and Dr. John Townsend, *How People Grow: What the Bible Reveals About Personal Growth* (Grand Rapids, Mich.: Zondervan, 2001), p. 228.
4. James Strong, *Strong's Exhaustive Concordance* (Gordonsville, Tenn.: Dugan,), p. 113.

CHAPTER 9

1. Scott Stanley, Daniel Trathen, Savanna McCain, and Milt Bryan, *A Lasting Promise: A Christian Guide to Fighting for Your Marriage* (San Francisco, Calif.: Jossey-Bass, 1998), pp. 59-61.
2. Ken Gire, *The Reflective Life: Becoming More Spiritually Sensitive to the Everyday Moments of Life* (Colorado Springs, Colo.: Chariot Victor, 1998), p. 46.
3. Dr. John Gottman and Nan Silver, *The Seven Principles for Making Marriage Work* (New York: Three Rivers Press, 1999), p. 17.
4. Eddie Ensley, as quoted by Sandra Wilson, Ph.D, *Into Abba's Arms* (Wheaton, Ill.: Tyndale, 1998), p. 33.
5. W. E. Vine, *Vine's Expository Dictionary of New Testament Words* (MacLean, Va.: MacDonald, 1993), p. 1180.

CHAPTER 10

1. Gary Thomas, *Sacred Marriage: What If God Designed Marriage to Make Us Holy More Than to Make Us Happy?* (Grand Rapids, Mich.: Zondervan, 2000), p. 93.
2. John F. Walvoord and Roy B. Zuck, eds., *The Bible Knowledge Commentary* (Colorado Springs, Colo.: Chariot Victor, 1983), p. 635.
3. Walvoord and Zuck, p. 637.

CHAPTER 11

1. Herbert Lockyer, *All the Women of the Bible* (Grand Rapids: Mich.: Zondervan), p. 236.

2. John F. Walvoord and Roy B. Zuck, eds., *The Bible Knowledge Commentary* (Colorado Springs, Colo.: Chariot Victor, 1983), p. 285.
3. Walvoord and Zuck, p. 285.
4. Gary Thomas, *Sacred Marriage: What If God Designed Marriage to Make Us Holy More Than to Make Us Happy?* (Grand Rapids, Mich.: Zondervan, 2000), p. 105.
5. Bill and Lynn Hybels, *Fit to Be Tied* (Grand Rapids, Mich.: Zondervan, 1991), p. 38.

ABOUT THE AUTHORS

DON AND JAN FRANK conduct marriage seminars across the country. Jan is a licensed marriage and family therapist in private practice. She has appeared on *The 700 Club*, *100 Huntley Street* (Canada), *Moody Radio*, and *Today's Family*. She has spoken at multiple conferences nationwide with regard to marriage, spiritual and emotional growth, abuse recovery and prevention, and developing intimacy with God. Don is a gifted communicator, coach, and mentor who loves to encourage husbands and fathers. He is currently a public school administrator. The Franks live in Placentia, California, and have two daughters in college.

If you would like more information about the ministry of Don and Jan Frank, you may contact them at:

P.O. Box 1491
Placentia, CA 92871
e-mail: don-janfrank@juno.com
web-site: www.janfrank.org